Hemingway
High on the Wild

Hemingway
High on the Wild

LLOYD R. ARNOLD

ILLUSTRATED WITH PHOTOGRAPHS

Grosset & Dunlap
Publishers • New York
A Filmways Company

Contents

1. Hemingway Comes to Sun Valley 1
2. The Family 33
3. "That Unshakable Hangover" 58
4. Mary Hemingway's Debut 79
5. The Good Postwar Fall 86
6. The Fall of '48 99
7. The Heiss House Fall 107
8. New Directions 116
9. A Stormy Season 141
10. The Short, Dark Fall of '60 149
    Epilogue 160

Acknowledgments

Acknowledgment is made to Ellis Chapin, to Lou Holliday, and to Ken Crabtree for photos made for this book in cooperation with the writer.

Dedication

To Tillie
and
In memory of my father, Bill

Foreword

The author was a good and true friend of Papa's over a span of twenty-two years. He has remained my friend and my family's for that long and more. Over the years of Hemingway peregrinations to Idaho, Lloyd's life was inextricably interwoven with ours, first as a photographer and fellow shooter, then increasingly, then permanently as a part of Hemingway life in Idaho.

This book is Lloyd's sympathetic and evocative testimony to an important facet of my father's life. He brings to it a well-founded understanding of the elements which go to make up a sportsman as well as a deep love and appreciation for a sportsman's country. Perhaps, most importantly, Lloyd's sense of humor and his Westerner's way of expression give to his book a very special quality of earthiness and of truthfulness.

HEMINGWAY HIGH ON THE WILD will stand, and well, on its own merits without the added dividend of a profuse and well-chosen collection of Lloyd Arnold's own photographs. I am happy that a small group of old and close friends gathered after Papa's funeral in 1961 and were more than right when they agreed that, to tell the story of "the way it really was" in Idaho, Lloyd Arnold was the one.

— John H. Hemingway

KETCHUM, IDAHO
March 21, 1968

1.

Hemingway Comes to Sun Valley

On a bright morning in the last days of the summer of 1939, I rode a spirited horse across the path of a big man and a tall attractive blond girl. My first glance at the strangers was a casual one, and necessarily brief. The man had a familiar look. When I lifted my hand in a little "Howdy, strangers" salute, he grinned broadly and returned it, snapping it off briskly as a sharp soldier would. The clues were obvious: the massive stranger in the neat but worn jeans, very flat-soled boots, wearing a fringed latigo leather hunting vest over a light shirt with rolled-up sleeves, was none other than Ernest Hemingway.

As Sun Valley's chief photographer, Lloyd R. Arnold would be partially responsible for this man's entertainment.

A lone car parked in front of the Sun Valley Lodge — a very dusty, current-model black Buick convertible — was a further clue to his identity. If the car had come from Montana by the most direct route, I was indeed familiar with the stretch of road that had made it look so travel-weary.

Just two words adequately describe Gene Van Guilder's and my first talk with Ernest Hemingway at Sun Valley: interestingly funny. To substantiate, I quote a later remark he made about it: "Who was kiddin' who and nobody kidded nobody."

I found Gene dressed for cocktails instead of in his usual Westerns, scolding himself a bit, for he had only had a look at Hemingway from his "hole" in the bell service desk in the lobby. Gene had been off the premises when Hemingway and his lady arrived well after dark the night before. Luckily, general manager Pat Rogers

1

Sun Valley in 1939.

happened to be in the lobby of the Sun Valley Lodge at the time, and put the pair in the best deluxe suite. Gene got word of it early the following morning. He called the Hannagan New York office and talked to Steve Hannagan's next-in-charge, who seemed mildly surprised that Hemingway had shown up. He did know, however, that Hemingway was due in Montana at roughly that time, and said he understood that Hemingway had told whomever contacted him that if things worked out right he might take a couple of days and drive over for a look at Sun Valley. Point-blank I asked Gene if he'd been offered a deal of some kind. He laughed and said, "What do you think?" Then with a rather sardonic grin on his handsome face he said that he'd been warned to handle the man with silk gloves — "he spooks easy." We retired to the far end of the lobby to await a signal from the maitre d' that the people had finished their meal. A point that troubled Gene was this: There was nothing but fishing going on, so how could we expect to hold this man who, Gene had been advised, was interested mainly in hunting, and who had a heavy writing program under way? A good question. For a quarter of an hour we schemed and planned. But I wanted to know who the girl was — she was not Mrs. Hemingway, whose picture I'd seen a few times. No, she was Martha Gellhorn, the writer responsible for the book *The Trouble I've Seen.* Did I know that the Hemingway marriage was on the rocks? No, I did not — I was a Hemingway follower mainly by reading him, not about him. My mind at the moment was on the hunt I had planned and I thought of Hemingway only as a big game hunter, from reading *Green Hills of Africa,* a favorite of mine.

2

When the maitre d' sauntered across the lobby, making little tents with his fingers and beaming his happy Bavarian grin, we knew that his lingual artistry was getting him by in fine style with Herr Hemingway; he called him a very funny man who talked about anything you liked. Karl Gebbert could fetch a laugh from a cigar store Indian. He said that Herr Hemingway had asked for the Hannagan man, but had fumbled in recalling his name.

"You go now, shentlemen." He grinned, but went on ahead so his absence would not be obvious.

Hemingway, at a table far back in the empty room, glued his eyes on us, and did not unglue them for an instant. At Gene's greeting he rose hastily and said, "Yeah, sure," and apologized for their lateness. He introduced "Miss Gill," who was perfectly at ease and who wore as infectiously pretty a smile as I'd seen in some time. There was an awkward moment of word fumbling all around, then she reminded Mr. Hemingway to ask us to sit down. A good idea. He grinned. A table was the place to talk around, easy on the feet and legs and something to lean on in support of your theories. He laughed heartily in support of his wit, finished it in a high-treble "Hmph!" and sat down while Karl slid chairs under us.

To open things Gene asked him if they had driven in by the south route or from the east. Hemingway eyed us both suspiciously, hedged a bit, grinned like a cat about to pounce on a mouse, and let us have it — straight. They came from the east, he said. He had always enjoyed the Park and he liked what he had seen of Idaho — very pretty country down the Snake River and west across the big Arco desert. The gaunt mountains to the north of the plain reminded him of Spain. Then, at our knowing nods, yes, right at dusk when you don't know whether to turn on lights and can't tell if you have, they had climbed the long easy grade that burst them suddenly upon the bleak, forbidding lavas of the

Bride-to-be Marty Gellhorn with her first loot taken with a gun.

Craters of the Moon National Monument. He referred to them as Dante's Inferno gone to sleep, and Mr. Dante's country — and Mr. Dante could damn well have it — and if he could have seen a place for a turnaround in that hell or purgatory they'd have headed back to Idaho Falls, had a few stiff ones, and said to hell with the great Sun Valley that he'd heard so much about. A sheepish grin ended it, then I got a half-startled glare for laughing outright. I told of coming through the Craters the fall before, blowing out a tire on the miserable gravel road, flattening a rear spring in the bargain, around midnight when it was black as pitch with coyotes off in nowhere calling for the moon. He howled gleefully and said, "Thanks ever so much."

In an apologetic aside, he went on to say that going back would have been a hundred miles to a drink and bed, he didn't see as owls do, and was not a record holder on any road. Besides, if a place like Sun Valley was so hard to get to there must be something here. He waved an arm toward outside, said he was now quite sure of it — a very pretty place, what little they'd seen.

Little formality was permitted from the outset — most evident by his quick dispensing with the "Mr." stuff, subtly, referring to himself as "old Ernie." We went along with this name-conscious man who of Gene's surname shyly said, "Dutch money is always solid." He mistook the short of my nickname when Gene introduced us, got it straight this way:

"That was much horse you rode out there . . . *mucho caballo*, my . . . uh, ah . . . how do they call you? Did we hear it as Pat?"

"No, it's Pap, or Pappy, either one." I had nothing in the flesh to justify it and

didn't mind much what I was called so long as it was in time for meals. Sure, said he, humanity generally finds the right one on the way up. Mine sounded all right. Did I mind if they joined the club, though my handle was a mild infringement on one of his? Hemming and hawing at my question about that, he was cut off by Miss Gill who said that his sons called their father Papa and that some of his cronies had picked it up. He thought it old-fashioned, she added, but one would have to be pretty thick not to recognize that he liked it. He *almost* blushed and I stifled my laugh; I said all old-fashioned kids used Papa, as I had until grown, then called my father Bill, as everyone else did.

"I like that," he said. "Like huntin' pals do."

He edged his way out of the "Miss Gill" business by referring to her as "the Marty," which seemed perfectly natural, and accused us of being Midwesterners from our speech. Miss Gill asked where, and said she, too, was from St. Louis. That's all there was. These people were Marty and Ernie to us.

A blind man could see that Ernest was impressed with Gene. He obviously knew he was in sheep country, which meant there were lots of Basque people — the original imported herdsmen — so the two got into both Spanish and the difficult Basque tongue. Obviously, most of it was unprintable. Listening to the guffaws, my impression was: This guy may be the great author Hemingway, but I like the big kid I see — a shrewd one, examining you subtly and carefully.

He was quite cagey when it came to the business at hand, and then ever so slowly he began to loosen up about it. Suddenly he gave it to us in a single package: He was not particularly interested in fishing — "too involving"; big game hunting was secondary because of the time element; but he understood that a man could have a lot of fun with a shotgun in our parts. Up to that point I had been mostly the listener, then

Gene said to Ernest, "Ask Pap about his surprise when he first saw it a couple of years ago." He grinned when in a half-question, half-statement, I said I might take him for an all-out shotgun man. I was fixed with his warm brown eyes while a forefinger bobbed in the general direction of his brow and he flatly said that of the few sports he truly liked he'd rather be a top wing shot than tops at any other. I said, "So would I," and that was all I said about it. He said he would like to see a little of our shotgun country at our convenience and if our time was short just give him a map — at reading maps, he was pretty good, he thought. Gene told him of his trip on the morrow, to firm up plans for a promotional potlatch dinner for sportsmen and outdoors writers to be held on Armistice Day, November 11, but said that he could easily put it off a few days. The old newspaperman responded instantly.

"Hell, no, don't put it off, Gene . . . wine 'em and dine 'em and they write the good stuff for you and it's more convincing from someone else, no matter how good you do it."

It was about nine-thirty when we sat down to talk, and the waitresses were checking their stations for lunch when Ernest broke it off, with apologies for taking so much of our time. Thanking us again, he said, "That's a pretty fancy wigwam that Mr. Rogers put us in over there . . . guess I'll have to do some stocking-up pretty soon."

After Gene got off a message to Hannagan about our publicity property we sat down to talk it over, and in the notebook that he slept with he put it all down.

"What do you call that way-out talk, Gene?"

"I guess you just add an *an* to his name . . . Hemingwayan."

"Get enough of it . . . Hemingwayana, huh?"

I wondered if we would get very much, and had a feeling that we just might. I offered to bet Gene that the trunk of the convertible was packed full. I wished that I had driven past it coming up from the stables to look for signs of a load.

Late that afternoon I was called to the general manager's office. Pat Rogers, whom we all referred to as the "Old Man," was in a fine mood, so I expected what I had heard many times in connection with special guests: "Feed 'em good, my boy, you never go wrong in that." My orders were to be available by phone from that moment on. When I showed Hemingway some country, I was to see to it that an ample pantry was aboard; the kitchen had been alerted and was at my command. Gene was there, quite bright-eyed, for he had spent an hour or so with Ernest in the Ram at a late lunch. He said iced tea laced with Scotch was a pretty fair drink, and that at sixteen ounces per, one was enough! He also threw me a curve.

"How would you like to take a fella named Hemingstein with you on your elk hunt?"

Who? Why, hell yes, I'd like to take him. Why not, he'd had lots of experience at it. The Old Man had okayed the trip — at company expense — and if Hemingway liked the sound of it, I was to invite him as our guest. In those days there was no elk hunting very close by; the animals were in the Selway Forest country far to the north, about the best on the continent, and it so happened that I was the only staffer who had been there. Taylor Williams was going with me and aside from pictures the Old Man wanted a pair of good heads to be mounted and hung on a pair of massive stone fireplaces in the new Trail Creek cabin, a mile up the valley. Ours was a big order. I asked Gene if he had learned anything else. He said no, he knew little more. Ernest had talked almost entirely of the goings-on in Europe — World War II was then just twenty days old — and had told Gene he was working on a novel based on the Spanish Civil War. When he left the next morning Gene told me that Ernest would call me.

My wife Tillie and I were barely out of bed the morning of September 22 when Ernest called about breakfast with us.

"Good morning, Chief. What a beauty Indian summer day."

"Just what the doctor ordered," I said. "But Indian summer? You know better."

"Yeah, the haze she's smoke from sagebrush fire somewhere . . . even bad Indian no allow that. . . ."

His squaw was sleeping still but he'd be right over, bring his pony, all loaded for the day's expedition. . . . Had I forgotten my promise to do the driving? "You can't look at new country with both hands full."

We looked for him in the lobby, but found him with a bellboy out by the big Village Square lagoon, helping him grain-feed the "wild" mallard ducks and the dozen-and-three family of Canada geese that fed from children's hands if their elders gave them a chance. Annie the antelope — the pretty lady that Taylor got from a rancher who'd found her as a tiny orphan — begged for a bite of grain. Ernest said that the ducks on the lagoon by the sun deck at Glamour House were his alarm clock that morning. "I came to, reaching for a gun." His exuberance was not the kind that rubbed off on you — he poured it on by the bucketful.

He'd gone to sleep on my *Idaho Encyclopedia* and had been absorbing it since first light. "A hell of a lot of state, this Idaho, that I didn't know about." We waited for Marty, talking in our room, me wondering when Ernest would ask where I planned to take them. My gear was in our huge closet and when I got it out, with hip waders included, he said, "I had a hunch, it smells of duck . . . I put ours in, too." Browsing in our modest but good-quality library he said he'd be honored to have a loan card — he lived so close by that he considered himself a good risk.

We spent the day in Silver Creek country, and the timing couldn't have been more right; the mourning doves were ganging up for the annual migration,

Hemingway holding snipe taken near Silver Creek, Idaho.

lingering in the abnormally warm weather to fatten on the abundance of the little wild sunflower seed. No stranger to dove shooting, Ernest forthrightly said he'd never seen anything to match their concentration. Driving slowly down a ruler-straight stretch of State 23 along the east high hills bordering the basin, we were lucky to catch the birds on the move to water following the morning feed; and like me, Ernest was flabbergasted that hunting pressure on our nation's number one game bird was nonexistent. He wished that he'd known it and come earlier. "Tuck it between our ears, Marty. Keep your fingers crossed for another fall." The basin supported a healthy balance of Hungarian partridge — a grand little upland bird — plenty of the big lumbering sage chickens, the largest of our native grouse. Both were good for the cause.

Ducks! They were the headliners. I chose a little used road on the slope of the south bordering hills, stopped on its high point where in a sweeping view some forty-odd square miles of shotgun heaven spread out before us. Confidently, I labeled it such, added "if there is such a thing, and if not, I think this will do until one comes along." Ernest nodded, got out his binoculars and put them to work. It was a near-windless day, not a duck in the air, but his ears told him the story, pointed his glasses for him.

Then the true exploration began, for we were directly above the joining of all feeder streams, looking down across a lush mile-square meadow, the main stream flowing through small ponds, their mirror surfaces dimpled by feeding lunkers — rainbow trout up to five and six pounds; mallard ducks dabbling along the tule-fringed banks in singles, twos, and threes. In his uninhibited elation Ernest asked which way would we go from there. The creek system was an open book to him so I said we'd look it over as such — from the beginning.

"Put your glasses on the big mile-square marsh about a mile due west, then look for a small slough of open water in its southeast corner . . . that's where we go next."

He had missed it since the flat angle of vision made the marsh appear as a long deep-green finger that might have fringed a stream. I considered it our first ace-in-the-hole. Ernest took a long look, lowered his

binocs, and never will I forget his look. That shallow slough was about three acres in size and its surface was black, and noisy, even at the distance.

"Jesus! Must be a thousand of 'em . . . big ducks, mallards, every one . . . this Marty must see, close up."

You could drive fairly close to it on a thread of old wagon road ankle-deep in alkaline dust, cut by shallow puddles of underground seepage. There is no mud known to man more slick than alkaline, but wheel ruts in the puddles were solid if the Buick's belly would clear. I hesitated. Ernest said, "I brought it to use." At the last of them, a long one, it looked too tricky; Ernest spotted a willow stick, said, "I'll walk the ridges and probe it . . . back off for a start . . . I wave, you come."

It worked, except that he waved a bit too soon, then just stood there; I had no choice but to floorboard it. The Buick roared on like a Cape Horner before a gale; the most I saw ahead was a leather vest sticking straight out behind, a big man in it, feet and legs a blur. He made it, barely, heaving like a blown horse when I pulled up on the dry.

"Quite a bit of speed you get out of that rusty knee, doctor."

"Funny what you forget when you damn well have to . . . and we didn't spook a duck — yet."

On a rise where the dim trail turned west, bordering the big marsh, I unlawfully spooked them off with a rifle I had brought along in case of an epidemic of coyotes, sent the bullet over their heads. While we drank a beer, "new" ducks dribbled back to the slough. But what he saw in the setup was its isolation and the difficulty of footing it across a quarter-mile flat of greasy mud — sharply calked soles were a must.

"Wanta try it?"

Damn right, he wanted to try it. With Marty between us, a mutual assistance thing, we made it. There hadn't been a hunter's blind on a strip of dry ground along the open water in years, though at some time an old hunter had contrived to raise it somehow.

"Probably with a team when it was frozen over," Ernest said. "Boy, it's a beauty deal, best I've ever seen, but if a four-legged critter ever went down on the flat . . . like a deer down on ice."

He asked if I'd ever used a machete. Would I cut off my own foot?

"Nothin' to it." He grinned. "Know where I can get the real thing, I'll send for a couple . . . no law against cutting sagebrush to make a couple of blinds with, is there . . . if we don't break our goddamn necks dragging it out here?"

As we slithered our way back, Marty said, "Gentlemen, I could write about this, and it would damn well be unprintable . . . title: 'Runny Nose Flat.' "

But down on a particular stretch of the main stream was the clincher: about a three-hour float trip — the cream of the wildfowlers' dish — jump-shooting from a boat. The beginning of it was at a highway bridge just thirty-two miles from Ketchum. We had squeezed in the time to run it a few times that summer, time it, figure it carefully — for our own use, naturally. Sure, we'd share it with ol' Ernie, and not noise it around, and there was only one man in the country who hunted it in a boat — a little one-man kayak. The entire run was within a privately-owned ranch where we had an "in" and our sneak boats were the canoes.

"The best," Ernest said, savoring the short bit of the stream visible from the bridge that looked placid and harmless. "If you know what you're doing . . . so open and handy."

Saturday morning we got Ernest and Taylor Williams together — a half-planned, half-accidental thing which Ernest went along with. He and I were tightening up his shotgun stock for some clay target shooting in the afternoon, working on the counter just inside the door of our shop when Gene and Taylor came. Seeing me fooling with a

gun was nothing new and Taylor paid no attention to the big man bent over on my off side. Instead, my wife Tillie was his target. He teased her about a trout dinner he'd promised her. The voice in back of me answered, "I heard that, Mr. Williams," then Taylor saw the face as it came up over

my shoulder. Mr. Williams didn't bat an eye, tipped his hat at talking angle, put out his hand, said there was a rumor going that he might show up some time — he *was* Mr. Hemingway, wasn't he? A single word describes their come-together: click! It was quite little while before the tomfoolery

Left to right: *Rancher Tom Gooding, Ernest Hemingway, Gene Van Guilder, and the author.*

took over, so we three waited until it came. Ernest was the trigger. He hinted quite strongly that his gunnery might win him the necktie that the colonel wore — hand-embroidered with trout fly patterns. The hell his gunnery might, the colonel said — that tie was a lady friend's gift and he wasn't getting it for money, marbles, or chalk!

On Sunday, September 24, Tillie and I got acquainted with another side of Ernest Hemingway.

On that first Saturday night on the town, when it was going good at the roulette wheel at the Alpine, he proposed a picnic for Sunday — on Silver Creek. Hadn't he said he was the biggest of all suckers for picnics? So Sunday morning, Ernest left his car for the gals to follow us in around noon with a picnic basket. I took down a station wagon to bring the canoe back. Ernest had not picked up a license of any kind, but Gene and I both had our rods along. Gene netted a couple of nice rainbow from a good stretch of water near the portage at Picture Bridge, about midway in the float trip. Lauding Gene's skill, Ernest again said that it would not do for him to get involved, though he did take my light rod and got himself a fair fish — "daudle fishing" in tennis shoes from the bank. Reading his thoughts, we spoke them for him. Sure, it would be great to take a little canoe run, plenty of time. I went for the boat and we put in at the last bridge — about a forty-minute float through an immense marsh of head-high rushes that we called the Chutes. Once in it you ran it all, no other choice, down to the pullout alongside the highway below Picabo.

On the stern paddle, where you get the true feel, Ernest saw at once that the creek wrote the rule book, you followed it, or else. A warm day, it was an oven in the Chutes, where the shooting would be sporting, but drop your birds in the stream. Nothing could retrieve a duck dropped in the impenetrable jungle walling the creek itself.

So, fishing was the lost subject, until in a deep pool a big rainbow as long as my arm rolled up alongside, took a look at us, impudently flicked his tail and moved on ahead.

"A friendly cuss," Ernest said.

"I doubt it, Ernie," Gene said. "He just came up to see what it is in his creek that's bigger than he is."

"I suppose you're right, Gene . . . a rainbow is a tuna is a whale."

A short silence, then: "And if either of you accuse me of a steal, accuse me of one that makes sense."

It made sense to get the hell on with the paddling — the mosquitoes and the gnats were eating us up. Chuck Atkinson met us with our station wagon, and over a beer with him at his store, plans for the afternoon were changed. We intended to take the lower route out of the basin and go south for a look at some pheasant country around Richfield, then on down near Shoshone where Gene had an errand. It was a rare day if you saw a pheasant around Silver Creek; too much snow in the winters. But they were on Ernest's mind, for we had seen a couple of them, drifters up from where they wintered, as were the ducks we'd seen. So, following our picnic under a big, lone cottonwood tree from which you could toss a pebble into the stream at Picture Bridge, we took the canoe to the upper bridge on the highway, for the full run. Outweighing me by a good forty pounds, Gene insisted that he and his wife Nin run his errand. They'd come by on their way back, about matching our time.

Well, a load we were indeed, for a light sixteen-foot craft: Ernest's two hundred-weight, Marty outweighing Tillie's hundred by too much, my scant one-fifty in the stern, where I insisted on paddling so the eager "gunner" could take the front view. In truth, we had a hell of a time balancing for a fairly level ride, and we very nearly rolled over getting under way. Damn fools, I thought to myself, and so did

Ernest, from the look he threw me over his shoulder. He spoke the truth when he said a canoe was a good part of his boating education. He was as good as any man I'd ever paddled with, and I could match him in all but the power in those huge shoulders and long arms, muscles rippling under a red plaid shirt.

Once under way we got along fine, and it would take a chapter to do justice to the delightful trip — isolation in a big flat pastureland where you felt you were off in another world, a thousand miles from nowhere. A healthy population of ducks nested and summered there in the little sloughs and marshes along the low banks, and they put on the show that Ernest was looking for. He made a cute response to an enraptured remark by Tillie. It was her first look at the basin. She loved the water anywhere (though she couldn't swim a lick), but had never experienced anything pertaining to hunting with me. On a sharp bend screened by a finger of tules we sneaked up on a few mallard drakes and susies that rocketed straight up in startled flight, washed Ernest's face in a spray of power-stroking wings, then, against an azure sky dappled with fluffy clouds, hung on their props like planes in the split second of leveling-out — a sight that veterans seldom see. Tillie gasped in delight, said, "Oh! Calendar ducks, just like what's-his-name would paint them for Brown & Bigelow."

Ernest turned his head, grinning his own appreciation, searched a moment for words.

"Yes, Tillie, weren't — they — beauties! Say . . . if you'll split that title with me I might do a piece on the calendar ducks . . . 'Ducks in the Afternoon.' "

On the upper half of the trip there were a number of obstacles: a low bridge or two, an abandoned irrigation flume, old moss-laden fence strands, and a shallow gravel-bottom cattle crossing a bit rough on our thin-soled feet. So we lightened the boat by getting out, slid it along with the girls in

it, our footing precarious on the slanting approach. I slipped and went to my knees a split second before Ernest did the same. He cursed outright, I called it "slick as hell, this four-letter stuff of cows that once was grass."

He let loose of the boat, stood upright, laughing like crazy, his eyes on the knees of his pants.

"Goddamnit, will you keep still till we get across this son of a bitch. . . . It'll be just our luck, Chief, to drop a duck on this s—— every time we run it."

Around four o'clock we eased out on the low grassy bank at pullout. Gene had left cold beer in the carryall. We split a couple and were about to load the boat to wait at Picabo. From there was a stretch of about four hundred yards, man-made to avoid the highway some fifty yards distant. No carrying of the boat; the car was parked a dozen feet from the bank — a fishermen's approach. At the end of the stretch was a sharp bend to the left, the stream disappearing in the walls of tules. From the road I knew there was an old decrepit place beyond the bend. Bud Purdy, the ranch manager, had said that an odd old geezer lived there, who raised turkeys and trapped muskrats in the big marsh for a living. A bridge in his yard crossed the stream, he had said; it might be a better place for a pullout. No, it was not a part of the big ranch, not much of anything as a property. The current was oil-smooth, but deceptively fast in the straightened channel. Should we chance it, see for ourselves? Ernest asked. I said no, for on either side of the canoe the name Sun Valley was painted in bright yellow letters — an odd old geezer might resent such an intrusion from the big plush place up north. But Ernest kept eyeing the water, and of course I went along — sure we could talk our way out at the bridge.

Using our blades only for steering, we went down at an alarming rate over bottle-green water. Near the bend there was a noticeable pull in the current; we heard the sound of falling water. We didn't glide around the curve, we shot around it, hugging the inside left. But for a low bank clear of tules, with little sagebrushes to grab, we'd have gone right over a two-foot-high fall — a rock ledge across the full width of the stream. Twenty feet beyond it was the bridge, so low a duck couldn't pass under it. A trap made to order for the old geezer!

On a patch of open ground about the size of a cabin porch he stood like a belligerent statue. His hands were tucked abib in old overalls, hip waders were rolled to his knees, there was a burlap sack at his feet and some traps. An old Army campaign hat shadowed his face, its brim snapped low, its crown pinched tightly fore and aft like those worn in the Spanish-American War. In the big yard beyond, on the bridge itself, was a solid sea of turkeys fattening for market. At our eye level it was a sea of red heads and necks — all talking at once. The statue remained glaringly silent at Ernest's friendly attempt at amenities. All four of us were hanging on for dear life, the prow actually hanging over the little fall. Ernest raised himself, got one foot on the bank, jackknifed with his stern skyward, then the statue came to life — audibly.

"Wh-wh-wh-wh-whatcha th-th-think yer g-g-g-gonna do?"

That explained a thing or two, but Ernest tried like a gentleman, got nowhere. Them turkeys didn't know strangers, disturbed their eatin'. I tried: it was a long pull back up that fast water. S-s-s-sure it was, but we came down it, we could go back up it. By then the air was charged, lightning silence before the thunder, then wham-o!

Ernest's behind hit his seat hard enough to break it, his paddle blade on the bank shot the prow broadside like from a catapult. He was a wild man forward, a Paul Bunyan on a rampage.

"Thanks for your g-g-g-goddamn c-c-c-courtesy! Stutter man, son of a bitch! Son of a bitch, stutter man! . . . And furthermore, you can take the goddamn

turkeys . . . no, by God, we should do it. . . ."

As we struggled against the tide I stole a split-second look at the old man before the bend cut him off from view. He had not moved a muscle. The fury in the boat was blowing itself out — we couldn't get enough air in our lungs, for clouds of gnats liked the sweat of our labors. Marty's sharp reprimand, shaky-voiced, brought the slowup to a halt — our anchor, handfuls of tall rushes. Tremulously, Tillie said, "Anybody wanta buy a turkey?"

"Jesus! Wasn't that an awful show I put on back there? I should drown in the sweat of shame for mocking the man. But damnit, he could have let us out. I'm sorry, Pappy, you called the turn, on the nose."

More than just a bit miffed at him, madder than a wet turkey at that overalled Horatio at the bridge, mad as two at myself, I said, "Shall we laugh and forget it, charge it to you-know-what?"

"Yes," Marty said. "If someone will tell me where he got that hat."

"Probably the old son of a bitch voted for the big T in Roosevelt." Ernest grinned sheepishly. "I couldn't tell whether he was forty or a hundred and forty . . . did he look at anybody else but me?"

No, not that we could see.

"Then, by God, I'm the spook, I guess."

We struggled on — like climbing the Matterhorn — Gene watching us from where we went astray: "Wait'll he hears about the turkey man, and Chuck and Bud, we'll get it with both barrels. If ever I suggest a move on something I'm a stranger to, just give me the hard tap one way or another."

We were not through with Stutter Man, nor he with us, by a long shot. Nor was Ernest hesitant in clearing the air for us while we loaded the boat. He said if Silver Creek's potentials were made to order for his working program, he was not a damn bit

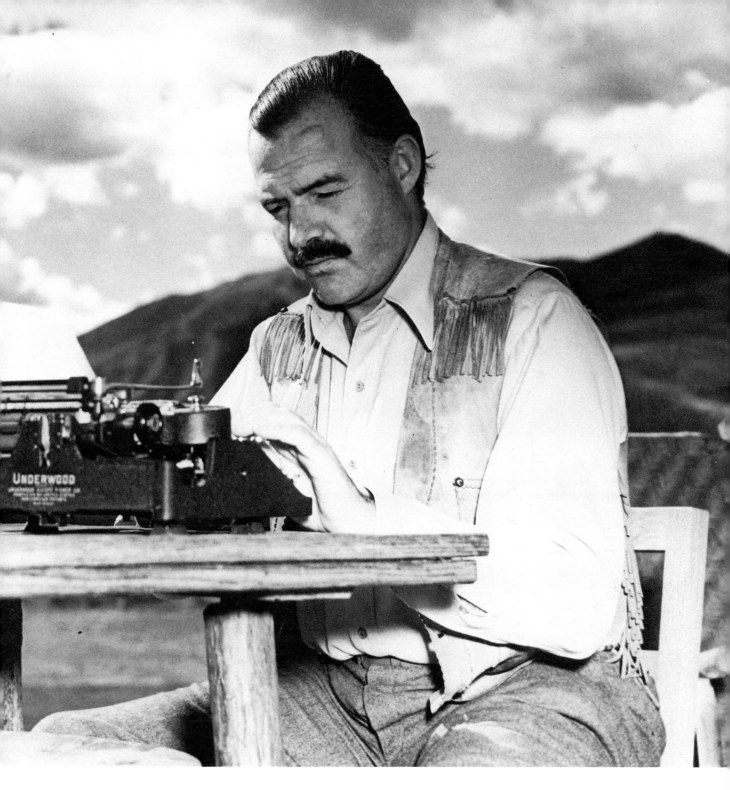

in doubt about the country's other offerings. Of course, it was a hell of a note that a man had to work with it dangling in front of him, but he guessed he could stand the wait for pheasants on October 15 and ducks on the twenty-second.

The work program started Tuesday morning, put off a day to go with us on a

At work on For Whom the Bell Tolls.

day-long trip to firm up plans with the packer who'd take Taylor and me after elk. He lived in the best of the Idaho antelope country, which Ernest wanted very much to see. The fleet pronghorn buck (the right name for the antelope) was a favorite with him, and when he said he had hopes for the following fall, some one of us said, "Fine, if we're not in the war up to our chins by then."

He said, "We won't be, I'm betting on it, long odds . . . but it's coming."

We left early Monday morning and our loop route through the very heart of the state's highest mountain country was one of rough, dusty, teeth-rattling roads. The worst of it was the old mining road at Sun Valley's back door, northeast over Trail Creek Summit, a hair-raiser, to put it mildly, and the very thing that appealed to Ernest when we started clawing our way up the canyon wall. In a word: unspoiled. He liked the immensity, the far-reaching look of the gaunt Lost River Mountains country. The

Good fishing on Silver Creek.

range itself was the state's roof, the one he had seen from the monotony of the Arco desert, reminding him of parts of Spain. Then when we wound down from a high Lost River pass into the upper reaches of the Pahsimeroi River Valley, he asked that we stop, give it a thorough casing from the distance of a high vantage point.

The Pahsimeroi is still off the beaten path, and in those days you heard of it in a way that suggested the mythical to an active imagination. It is old Indian country, the

A photograph taken by the author which was subsequently used for the dust jacket of For Whom the Bell Tolls.

western hunting range of the Shoshonis. Its musical name is legendary, sprung from the oddity of a small stand of pines along the river where the nomadic Shoshoni set up their lodges for the fall hunt. The trees did not belong in the aridity of that vast high valley, so the red man revered the region as sacred. Ernest thought it had an indescribably different look about it, and that it was also a bit of Spain in our hemisphere, the likes of which he hadn't seen before.

The special "permit-by-drawing" hunt opened the next morning, September 26, so, undisturbed, little bands of antelope were everywhere, some close, some far; down valley in the scattered ranch hayfields the "Pahsimeroi beef" helped themselves along with the cattle.

"I'm hooked, men," Ernest said. "Glad you got good connections in this country . . . we old Shoshonis will see it again."

In the little one-street dusty town of Challis on the Salmon River we met Bill Hamilton — a rawhide, pine-knot character epitomizing the sprawling, five-thousand-square-mile Custer County. One of a vanishing breed of men of whom Ernest said in the car when we recognized Bill's oxbow legs moving him along like a sore-toed rooster, "From here he looks the guy you'd go anywhere with in the mountains and he'd make it good for you whether you connect or not."

Gene or Taylor yelled at Bill, who threw us a toothless grin, yelled back, "Tie it 'n' git down, bin waitin' fer you birds long enough."

"I guess that's Hamiltonian, gents, for 'Park the buggy, old cowboys don't like to drink alone,' and I say he's not about to."

Ernest wore his old round-toed cowboy boots; otherwise he was dressed as when I had first seen him, with the addition of his big, battered old Stetson worn Afrikaner style — floppy brim, high pinched crown, tipped well back off his forehead. Bill kept eyeing it and shortly asked Ernest what part of the West he hailed from.

"Montana . . . when I'm lucky," he said. "I mean that's the part of the West I use mostly, Bill."

Bill had the name pegged all right, but walking down to a little bar, he suddenly looked up at this big Westerner who hadn't satisfied his curiosity.

"Ernie, you write Westerns?"

No words to describe Ernest's face, or ours, when he jerked his head around, grabbing at his falling hat.

In a small cafe where very long talk was made, and short work of some delicious grass-fattened steaks, Ernie got his other little gem of the day. The single waitress was a buxom, jolly gal who obviously knew how to fork a horse as well as hay, and butcher out what fell to her rifle, too. The writer of Westerns was right at home, so in joking about how rough the going was where he just might go with Bill, he told her it could be too much for him — he hadn't had much experience.

"Oh, don't worry, mister," she said matter-of-factly. "You're big enough to get yourself an elk with a stick."

He fumbled a bit in his retort to that one, and when she turned away: "Best compliment I've had since I was invited to the White House."

We took the Salmon River route home, the graveled Highway 93 hugging the river through the scenic heartland of the state for a hundred miles — to cross it as a tiny creek at the foot of Galena Summit, an hour from Ketchum. It would be hard to find a more satisfying hundred miles than following the storied River of No Return to its trickling source. Looking back on it from a high switchback on the snaky old Summit road, Ernest said softly, "You'd have to come from a test tube and think like a machine to not engrave all of this in your head so that you never lose it."

The following dawn the work on the novel continued as scheduled, we learned at a lingering lunch, and it went better in mountain cool than it had in months of heat in a hotel in Havana. He said he was on the rough of Chapter 13, and had worked the name Sun Valley into it. We lifted brows. How could he do it, time-wise?

He grinned. "The freedom of fiction."

As September drew to its close, Gene put out his first release to the press — on

Ernest fishing. A fishing trip was organized soon after with Pop Mark to act as guide. He selected Big Wood River below Magic Reservoir, splendid water for nice rainbow trout. There was a bug in that deal, though. In a grove of cottonwoods a short way upstream from the action, a very dead critter made the air thick enough to cut with a knife. The stench was almost unbearable, but the place was right. I got one action shot of Ernest fighting the fish, and on the posed shots, Gene stood by with a red bandana handkerchief tied over his face, just his eyes twinkling above it. Ernest burst out a big guffaw, said, "For Christ's sake, Jesse James, fetch the bottle of Scotch."

Jesse had it in his hip pocket, tipped it up under his mask for a swig, and passed it around. We did the rest of our fishing at Timmerman Dutch Charlie's place on our way home.

The date was September 28, the one and only time that Ernest seriously fished for trout in Idaho. He told me later that the "come hell or high cow" episode had about closed the book on his freshwater fishing, and that the action picture was the only one of its kind in existence.

Ernest went along with Marty's fondness for riding. He rode quite well himself, though his sitting a horse might be described as rather "leaden" or deadweight. Gentle with his mount as if it were a kitten, he didn't rate equine intelligence very high, an observation he'd make with a hearty laugh: he figured the horse was damn well aware of it. Perhaps so, for every mount that Bob Miles picked for him (a different one each ride) was not a good match. Ernest was one of those people who made a horse nervous. Bob's ranch foreman and boss of all things horse, Spike Spackman, accused him rather flatly of running his horse excessively, which was not the case at all. But it was done good-naturedly, and finally Spike's horse sense solved the problem.

In some one hundred and twenty-five head there was one that could do the job: a

Hemingway and Gene Van Guilder, Union Pacific's P.R. chief at Sun Valley, on the trap-shooting range.

gray chunky horse named Antelope who let nothing bother him. He was a risk horse, something of a clown, and had been used by movie units from Hollywood — Sun Valley country was then quite in demand for locale. Ernest became buddies with Antelope, rode him up the big mountain·with Gene and me — a five-hour ride — with no trouble at all. And he learned something about Antelope's high rating. In the spring of '38 the opening scenes of the fine motion picture *Stanley and Livingstone* were shot out of Sun Valley, in the Boulder Mountains ten miles north, with Spencer Tracy and Walter Brennan. One of them rode Antelope in the scenes showing the great reporter covering the Indian fighting in the West.

Riding along happily one afternoon, Ernest said, "By God, ol' Ernie's gittin' up in the world, riding Spencer Tracy's horse. But, Antelope, actors are phony, writers are phony, and I think we can class you as a phony, too . . . any minute you just might unwind and pitch ol' Dr. Hemingstone in the sagebrush, flat on his ass."

Dr. Hemingstone never suffered such an indignity, nor would he allow me to include him in an informal picture of the riding tribe — six of us. But something came out of the riding. North of town on the west of Big Wood River, is Adams Gulch, very pretty country dominated by a high, rocky, timbered butte of the same name. Ernest spotted the area before we rode into it with him for the first time. He said that it would be ideal if his current work should sometime be produced as a movie. We rode in the big gulch several times, high up to look it over thoroughly; then, since Bob Miles was responsible for Hollywood's interest, Ernest suggested that come spring we photograph Adams Gulch in light

lingering snow — have the pictures on hand in case. It was a shy suggestion, but movie locations were a lucrative business for the resort. We assured him we'd do it.

Right up to almost the last minute, Ernest counted on going with us after elk. He bought his general license, an elk and a deer tag, had a saddle scabbard made for his Springfield, and bought mountain boots. We sighted-in our rifles on a rainy Sunday afternoon, our takeoff slated for early Tuesday. Like me, his concern was for Taylor who had been ill, for whom it could be an ordeal. Openings of elk seasons are famous for sudden early storms. I assured him that Taylor was well aware of his limitations due to his setback and that I could handle his pride in holding up his end if the going got rough. On Monday afternoon he came by the shop and asked me to come to Glamour House for a thorough rundown on the situation as I saw it. That had an odd ring, for we had gone over it plenty; there had to be another motive.

A procrastinator of the first class, Taylor had ordered himself a heavier-caliber rifle for the big deer that, oddly enough, he had not hunted in his years in the West. In error, or as a substitute, the model 70 Winchester came with an open-notch sight mounted well forward on the barrel. His own model 70, in identical caliber to my light rifle for antelope and deer, was equipped with the receiver-mounted aperture sight close to his eye; of the old school, he had not yet taken to 'scopes. The air turned blue around him; he would take it anyway and be handicapped. Then Ernest took advantage. I know there were sincerity and disappointment in his back-out: he was in correspondence with his editor at Scribner's, Maxwell Perkins. Walking to the Lodge he told me that he intended sending his Springfield .30-06 with Taylor, if he had to take him down and sit on him for agreement. He called him over in a while, made a big to-do of driving home the fact

that bullets are like medicine — if a little is good, more is better: a 130-grain pill was not enough medicine for a big dangerous critter, his 180-grains would leave no doubt about a cure. In those days there was "status" in a hunter owning a custom-built Springfield by such masters as Griffin & Howe, and the colonel was reluctant to take it. He stood as much chance as a snowball in hell. The one gun that Ernest really cared for was thrust upon him, and that was that. It had served its owner well, and it was good Indian sign — even old witch doctor Hemingstein backed up the medicine man in that. He went into his bedroom and returned with a small leather pouch bag about the size of two clenched fists — a primitive thing that had been around a long time. Pawing around in it, his fingers turning up things that our curious eyes scarcely believed, he fished out a good-luck piece for me, and watched while I buttoned it safely in my shirt pocket.

"You have to shoot pictures, too, Pappy. Sorry I don't have anything in that line."

His grin was straight, and I said, "Hell, who of us doesn't draw on the squatting around a fire in a loincloth instincts buried deep within us?"

"Hmph! Anybody who says he doesn't. . . ."

The colonel took off in a high lope, said he'd be back in an hour; I said to Ernest, "Three guesses, and your first is the right one."

Yeah, he guessed he'd call the tribe for the shindig; and the old Kentuckian outdid himself, if such was possible, with the mint juleps that he had glasses being frosted for. No one ever figured just how he managed so late in the growing season to produce those heavenly mint sprigs when by all the rules they should have been strong. They'd be even better, he'd say, if his mint was grown on the shallow grave of an old Confederate soldier. Was he damn sure he hadn't lifted one complete and transplanted it in Idaho?

"Christ! This is good, how long before a man can't get up and walk out by himself?"

The colonel had finesse, and restraint: you had one, plus a small dividend, and you knew you had been on a journey!

With plum jubilee for dinner dessert, we wondered if we'd make an early rising — three o'clock — for the long drive into Montana, then back across the high pass into Idaho to our road's-end camp. We made it with a further send-off: still leery of our success in the dry, overly warm weather, Ernest got out of bed, threw a trench coat over his pajamas and robe, and came over to the Inn square where we'd parked our loaded carryall; not only to send his regrets to Bill Hamilton, but to admonish us again not to leave the "delicacies" when we butchered-out the big wapitis we were sure to get, one way or another. I can say with feeling that as our lights stabbed a hole in the stygian black on the summit road out of the valley, we felt the old Indian's presence. Maybe he upped good fortune in another form, too — Bill Hamilton could blow an elk bugle made of a hollow stick to make your nape hairs stand on end — the rut was still on and there was much music in the Selway.

On Sunday afternoon about four — after six days absence — I backed our car to the Inn kitchen dock to unload a thousand pounds of meat in quarters with the hide on, in perfect condition for curing; two above-average antlered heads skinned out and caped for taxidermy, two growths of whiskers and strong smells about us. We'd left the Selway in the wee hours; the colonel slept most of the way home. But now as I saw to unloading, he warmed up reporting in to the Old Man, and was on high C when he phoned Glamour House. The doctor was in, but we'd have to leave our whiskers on to prove that we'd been out in the hills, let alone back so soon. (We'd knocked four days off our estimate.) But we'd clean up otherwise, then be over. A hell of a good idea. The doctor laughed — he'd been elking a time or two. If we didn't clean up,

any stray dogs around the place might swamp us!

The colonel's pleasure was the first order of business: He fished from his pocket the single deformed bullet we'd dug from his nice big bull — dropped as if pole-axed when hit high in the neck at three hundred yards with the strange rifle and iron sights — remarkable shooting under the stress of labored breathing and hard stalking. We verified the yardage with the range finder on my camera. Ernest was as exuberant as if he'd made the shot himself.

"I told you, I told you, Colonel, that you could shoot that rifle, didn't I now?"

I gave him back his good-luck charm — the bullet that had killed his first Wyoming elk, its copper jacket now green with age, but a bit pocket polished on the high spots — and I had a single bullet, too, from my first elk. He ran me down, almost, on a dim trail that I couldn't get out of, spooked to high heaven by Taylor's shot, so mine was in self-defense.

"And did you make like pup not broke to house?"

"What do you think, Doctor . . . he looked the size of a locomotive."

He bled with us in our tale of having to walk out of the country some eighteen miles, leading our packed saddle horses, because of the sudden, vicious, wet snowstorm that gummed up the works by stranding half our pack string supplying another camp. We walked out to save our meat from the thaw warm-up that followed immediately. Ours was a trip worthy of writing up.

Did we bring all the "goodies" as promised? Yes, Bill said to tell ol' Ernie that he took care of them himself, from hearts to nuts, and the rest was up to us — get the hell for home once we got out to base camp through that knee-deep snow.

"Well, great. Guess I'll have to check over the livers good when we go over to eat . . . might want to trade mine in on a new one."

Should he put that in the story, Gene asked.

"Sure, I know an outfit or two who'll pay extra for that item."

The complexion of things changed when the colonel fixed the doctor with a steely eye behind a leveled finger and told him that the magic, voodoo, whatever the hell he called it, that he dispensed in the guise of good-luck wishes was damned suspicious — every possible eventuality talked of had come to pass. He got his laugh for all the good, and the feeling for the bad. The old boy was purple-faced with exhaustion from that walkout that as the kid of the trio I broke trail for. He scared the wits out of Bill and me, that remarkable piece of human rawhide who waited a long time that night before sipping a small hot toddy.

The other was an item to get the ear of any old mountain hunter. When packing in the meat to our hunting camp Bill and I had a thrill: a magnificent big bull in his prime, his nose full of the scents from the loads our weary horses carried, wanting to fight, blowing, stamping his feet, at some fifty yards against a mist-shrouded canyon. With a neutral void as a background, this was a picture the mind's eye sees but once in a lifetime of hunting. Bill threw a stick at him and yelled an insult, and the regal old boy slowly turned and ambled out of sight. I said to Bill, "Didn't he remind you of the trademark on Hartford Insurance Company calendars and ads?"

"I think he was an even better one," Bill said. "Not doctored up by a paintin' feller who prob'ly never seen one where he belongs."

"Aren't you glad you had yours on the horses?" Ernie said. "He's the kind that's good to leave for seed . . . let's hope nobody gets him."

Nothing to do when we went to dinner but to inspect the loot in the cooler boxes; the Old Man with us, and big Ray Daly, a cook who did marvelous things in his smokehouse. Then out in the service hall,

where our group stopped to listen to Ernest extol the virtues of a smoked elk sandwich in a future duck blind, a lady guest who knew all us staffers very well gave us the treatment, greeting the assembly, "Why, Mr. Hemingway, this must be an occasion for something."

"Yes, lady, it's an occasion, all right. Our friends are back from a successful trip, and we are happy about it."

Well, from our collars up, Mr. Williams and I were badgers, not men, and the old basking biddy said, "Why, I have missed you two since we came the other day, have you been prospecting?"

"No, Mrs. we've been hunting elk."

"Why, of course, it *is* the season, how stupid of me. Did you catch one?"

The Old Man had ducked like a scalded cat through the Ram door and Mr. Milquetoast was edging away. A long arm went about Taylor's and my shoulders and the hissing voice close to our ears said, "Yes, they caught two, would you like to see them? . . . They come in five pieces each, with the hair on."

Swish! Skirts through the closest exit.

At the table: "Did you *catch* one? Obscenity! Why that old counterfeit would think your Hartford elk was a goddamn kangaroo."

By then, having worked quietly at his mail and phone, Gene's euphoria for his November affair was at high level — high attendance was assured; he had fish salted away, smoked sturgeon from the Snake River, — and he hoped that we of Sun Valley could round out the bill of fare when the bird shooting opened. It was warming to witness Ernest's pleasure in Gene's satisfaction, and you liked the sincerity of him saying, "Sure, I'll make a speech of no more than six words — if you write it, Gene." Through an odd quirk of reporting by a fellow staffer, Taylor and I sneaked out at daylight two mornings after our return and brought in two fat young deer, taken a half-hour's ride away. We tried to get Ernest to go, but he said, "You guys get 'em, thanks ever so much . . . I'm on a good stretch in the running and I can't let loose of it."

Ernest and Gary Cooper met by telephone. Coop had promised the previous spring that he'd do all possible to make it that fall. However, a film materialized. In later communication on another matter, Coop said that he might make it for a few days of hunting, around the time of the potlatch affair. Ernest was in camp when Gene got the last word from him, so with all of us in a gay mood Gene proposed that he write Coop a letter advising him of Ernest's presence, write the letter "in quad" as he dubbed it, suggesting that Ernest sign it with Gene, Taylor, and myself. He said sure he would, didn't Mr. Cooper owe him a drink or two — he'd contributed to his career in a small way, hadn't he? In the morning Gene thought differently of it and I said if he said he would, he'd sign that letter gladly. He did: "It looks like a good booking up here, try and get a piece of it with us. E. H."

Exactly a week later, when we were at dinner in the Ram, Coop called. He was fairly sure that he couldn't make it, but there was a vague chance. When we all had a few words with him, Gene waved the instrument to Ernest, who came without a second's hesitation, with a shy grin and a bright crack. But he was taken with the nice voice, its easygoing, shy buildup to a stranger.

"Sure unwinds with the talk when he gets going," he said.

Looking at his watch, the colonel quipped, "About four bucks worth of his money. Coop writes letters like a bald man uses a comb."

Fate's docket had it that they would not meet in the flesh in the lovely fall of '39.

Old waterfowlers never get too excited when the season opens. You take a few local ducks, they say, to satisfy the appetite and wait for weather to bring down the northerners. So it was with us that fall: more parties shooting than were counted on — and the locals were quickly scattered. Ernest was more than happy with a couple of runs on Silver Creek. Then, coming up from pheasant shooting one night, with a few ducks in the loot, he handed Gene a press agent's gem: He'd write an article on Idaho's great shotgunning; he knew he could plant it for winter publication with his good friend Arnold Gingrich at *Esquire;* make it long enough to run as a series of two or three. Great, Gene said, but for heaven's sake, not at the expense of his regular work. Hell no, he said, he could tuck it in.

The idea grew with Gene, a natural that brought the Snake River into the picture. There was something of a novelty, when conditions were right, in Hagerman Valley. Taylor knew it like the palm of his hand, so Gene called him to describe it to Ernest. Sure, he said at once, it was entirely possible to shoot both ducks and pheasants on river islands and along the east bank that was a veritable jungle of cover where the long mile of waterfalls plunged into the river. "But," he said, "it can work hell out of you, too."

He knew what he was talking about, and the valley with its "Thousand Springs" aquatic display is a lovely scenic attraction — right alongside the highway. From it came the suggestion to take a day of the October 28–29 weekend to look it over. "Sure, make a picnic of it, take the gals along, see something we haven't seen before."

But it didn't work out that way, and Gene was unduly worried about a shortage of ducks for his potlatch. The result: we took our wives for the outing, a canoe, and, for an extra gun and license, a willing young man on the staff. He hunted birds regularly with Pop Mark, paddled a canoe well, and talked hunter's language. We left Friday afternoon, intending to return Saturday night. Saturday was scarcely worth the effort, but the potential was there, and we decided to stay over for at least a try at it Sunday morning. We were set well enough in a little tourist cabin layout; Gene called Ernest, who said he still liked what he heard — we'd set it for the next weekend, hoping for some good old-fashioned duck weather in the meantime.

Sunday was worth it, and by about one o'clock we called it quits, a few birds short of our limits.

While we paddled the half-mile up the west shore, ducks started to stir, raised by a distant pleasure boat. I paddled stern, Gene forward — it was his turn to shoot if something passed close enough to a little tule-fringed bay we ducked into. Our companion, whom I'll call Dee, was the midship passenger, having finished a fair morning in a makeshift blind on one of the islands. Something did come along shortly, drifting down on the water, dabbling busily along the low tules. Gene thought the little ducks were teal, the best of eatin' ducks, bar none; the backlight glaring the water fooled him. When in easy range they skirted the low tules concealing us — buffleheads, little diving ducks — I said, "Let 'em go, Gene." My voice didn't raise them, and I thought he would let them go. Then, tightly bunched, they took off, straightaway, and Gene fired both barrels, in normal succession. Six birds down, but two were winged only, and under they went.

"Now we have some chasing to do, mark 'em. . . ."

I was cut off by a violent roll of the boat, a sharp thud on its bottom, a single shot — out of the river a cripple surfaced where I thought he would — a silence, an ominous silence! Look, look! Something went wrong, boy! I looked, and I saw, clearly, in an instant. Poor Gene had triggered it himself, a series of tragic errors.

To flush the ducks, and shoot, he stood fully upright in the narrow prow, without feeling the slightest movement of the boat.

In easing himself down, he turned to grasp the gunwale with his right hand, his gun held high in his left. He was frozen in this half-turned, half-crouched position when my horrified eyes saw the hole just under his right shoulder blade. The smoking muzzles of Dee's double-barreled 12-gauge were directly in line, its buttstock resting on the

Mallard ducks wintering on Snake River.

canoe's ribs, held by its grip. Then I knew
that the shots downing the ducks were
singles from both guns. Recoil upset Gene's
precarious balance, the lurching boat upset
the rest.

There's an old unspoken rule governing
the shooting from a boat: Unless in a solidly
anchored and specialized craft, it's a

one-man show — period. Weapons other than his are put aside — empty.

No mortal power could save Gene, and the best I could do was make him as comfortable as possible from his fall into the boat while Dee tore for help toward a group of men in a farmyard some distance downstream. The wait of fifteen minutes was eternity; and I've never ceased to wonder at the courage and honesty in the remarkable man who was Gene Van Guilder. He had a number of things to say, and we managed them all, some nearly as hard to pass on, and try to carry out, as watching him die. It came quietly — in the shade of the little farmyard about two o'clock.

Now the old pro had to put aside the hurt and go to work. The closest town was twenty miles upriver to the south; there was no difficulty with the coroner, the reporting to the sheriff — both were friends of Gene. I had Nin's confidence, so I went ahead with all arrangements, mindful of the hundred-mile distance from home. Tillie handled the messages by calling them to Sun Valley. The Old Man was absent and at my suggestion she called him about the potlatch dinner. Cancel it, was his immediate decision; without its architect it wouldn't be any good. In the interim, Ernest was alerted and the first thing he asked me was "Can I handle the newspapers for you?" Indeed, he could, I had everything at tongue's tip, then warned him that the flash news would be on the radio shortly, there could be a deluge of phone calls. Put it out of mind, he said, he was in the hotel office with Flo Reilly, had called Taylor, who was standing by. He had correctly guessed that all our gear and birds had been left in our haste at the river place, and time was the need now — get home. The stuff would be sent for first thing in the morning.

All of this a roundabout way of saying that in harsh criticism of myself back there on the river, I hardly knew how to begin. It was like talking to my father, a mountainous man when you were in trouble.

With others there for the follow-through, he was waiting for us on the Inn porch at eight o'clock, between phone calls, and he'd scarcely been off it in the two hours since I'd talked to him. The messages to company officials still had to be dictated and sent immediately, so he helped us in wording them. By then, the tension was beginning to unwind and he came to our room for a short while, when our first bite since breakfast helped to stem it. He said good night, after asking if I would have breakfast with him and we'd talk good. Up to then I wouldn't have bet very much on him sticking around — for the obvious reason, and another.

Shortly before, we had learned that Marty had been angling for a European war assignment with *Collier's*, had landed it, and was waiting for word to leave. Ernest sensed what was on my mind and promptly said he was not going anywhere. He was both sympathetic and very severe about the rule-breaking, the bad gun-handling.

"So, how can we call it anything else but impulsive action? No, you and Gene were a fine team, and didn't go about telling each other what to do, and I admire your stand, but I won't buy it. If you insist, I'll take the stand with you . . . I'm involved, too."

A phone call from Gary Cooper broke it up; when I finished, Ernest talked with him at length; they made a tentative date for the next fall. Then, walking down to the shop with me, he said, "Now, you have lots to do and I'll stay out from under your feet, but I'm going to check in with you, my way . . . you won't mind, will you?"

No, I wouldn't mind at all; my first task was to write a letter to Steve Hannagan, and I figured it would take the rest of the day. A noble thing to do, Ernest said, a must, so I said I might check in with him for approval of what I wrote. He said, "Sure, kid, we're going on as best we can."

He checked it the following morning, approved it, and said he had struggled with something very difficult to write, too — since dawn and part of the night before. I knew what it was; Nin had told me that she had asked Ernest to write a tribute to Gene, and read it at his funeral. He was glad to do it, but humbly said, "Gee, I wish that I could redo it for someone else to read . . . I'm no good in crowds, I don't talk well, kids, you know that."

He had it with him, typed on onionskin paper, rolled as a narrow scroll, and asked us to read it, see if we thought it "too flowery." We were glad that he turned to look at pictures, but as we went along, its sheer perfection and fitness overwhelmed our tears. Tillie handed it back to him, said, "Papa, it's beautiful."

We buried Gene in the shabby little Ketchum cemetery on the clear, warm afternoon of November 1. In firm, steady voice, Ernest Hemingway read his tribute to the man he'd known but a short six weeks:

You all know Gene. Almost everyone here is better equipped to speak about him and has more right to speak of him than I have. I have written down these thoughts about him because, if you trusted yourself simply to speak about Gene, there might be a time when you would be unable to go on.

You all know that he was a man of great talent. He had great talent for his work, for writing and for painting. But he had something much more than that. He had a great talent for living and for communicating his love and enjoyment of life to others.

If it was a fine bright day and you were out in the hills with Gene, he made it into a better day. If it was a dark gloomy day and you saw Gene, he made it a lot less gloomy. There weren't any bad days when Gene was around. He gave something of himself to all those who knew him or worked with him. And what he gave us all was very precious because it was compounded of the rarest elements. It was made up of true goodness, of kindliness, of fairness and generosity, of

good humor, of tolerance and of the love of life. What he gave us he gave for good.

We have that from him always. When I heard that Gene had died I could not believe it. I cannot believe it now. Yes, technically he is dead. As we all must be. But the thing he gave to those who knew him was not a thing that ever perishes and the spirit of Gene Van Guilder is not a thing that will perish either.

Gene loved this country. He had a true feeling and understanding of it. He saw it with the eyes of a painter, the mind of a trained writer, and the heart of a boy who had been brought up in the West, and the better he saw it and understood it, the more he loved it. He loved the hills in the spring when the snows go off and the first flowers come. He loved the warm sun of summer and the high mountain meadows, the trails through the timber and the sudden clear blue of the lakes. He loved the hills in the winter when the snow comes. Best of all he loved the fall. He told me that the other night riding home in the car from pheasant hunting, the fall with the tawny and grey, the leaves yellow on the cottonwoods, leaves floating on the trout streams and above the hills the high blue windless skies. He loved to shoot, he loved to ride and he loved to fish.

Now those are all finished. But the hills remain. Gene has gotten through with that thing we all have to do. His dying in his youth was a great injustice. There are no words to describe how unjust is the death of a young man. But he has finished something that we all must do.

And now he has come home to the hills. He has come back now to rest well in the country that he loved through all the seasons. He will be here in the winter and in the spring and in the summer, and in the fall. In all the seasons there will ever be. He has come back to the hills that he loved and now he will be a part of them forever.

When the casket was lowered to ground level, kindly Ab Womak put on it the hand-stamped saddle he'd made for Gene, hooked his silver-mounted bridle and spurs on its horn. The old man's eyes were misty and his toil-worn hands trembled as he covered these things with the saddle's blanket, then bewilderingly turned, as if lost. He had put down his hat while at his task, forgot it, but the big young feller in the old hunting jacket two sizes too small for him picked it up and handed it to Ab. And so, we were seven as the shovel was passed from hand to hand.

In our time together I had covered a lot of ground with Gene Van Guilder and I knew that he had a host of friends. It seems that we were close to an hour talking with them — of the good things that were. As said, the little burial ground was not much in those days, typical of so many detached communities. But somehow the neglect of the living seemed not to matter in the serenity of the big land itself — "In all the seasons there will ever be."

We had walked the mile over from the Lodge so we walked back, up the gentle slope of the cutoff road past the cone of little Penny Mountain. Near the crest of the low pass we stopped, automatically, I suppose, to look back where the big mountain's shadow line halved the valley in the bright light of day and the gray of evening, the silence toned by the murmur of the distant river.

"You know, men, we let Gene down a little today . . . as long as something had to be sent with him, we should have put in his ax, his rod, and his frying pan."

"And six-gun to knock off a fool hen for change," the colonel said. "But he won't hold it against us until we get there."

"No, the opposite . . . now do we each turn around to the other for a swift kick?"

Sounds a little rough — yes — but true; a practical expression of feeling, understanding, for those left in the game — backed by a mountain of waiting generosity. No one turned around; we walked on to meet an old friend of Gene's who'd come over from Boise — a man I'd met that summer. Taken with him, Ernest asked him to come to his place and we'd talk.

We recall our greatest sensation that fall as the privilege of reading twenty-four chapters of *For Whom the Bell Tolls* directly off the typewriter. Up to this offer, Ernest had seldom mentioned the big work. We kept hands off, but we learned a couple of its characters' names this way:

On one of the Adams Gulch rides, Ernest called it "El Sordo country." Then long later he came to lunch in an ebullient mood and Tillie said, "Papa, you're in fine fettle, it must have gone good this morning."

He laughed, said, "Yes, Tillie, it did. Now you take Pablo, for instance, I haven't known what the old son of a bitch is gonna do from one day to the next, but finally I got him figured out . . . it isn't going to be good, and I wouldn't want him doing it to me, I can tell you that. . . . Would you guys like to read it?"

"Would we?" Taylor said. "When do we start, Mr. Author?"

Mr. Author grinned, replied, "Well, you should tell me to go to hell, but I guess a few stanzas of it when you're ready just might lead to that."

Our installment reading was done at night, propped up in bed, the twenty-fourth chapter finished in early December. As we went along it was obvious that the hero's reference to his father's suicide was based on facts in the author's life — of which we still knew so very little. Then one evening when we were just in from hunting, Tillie came to Glamour House to join us in a drink, and brought a sheaf of the manuscript that we'd finished. We were in a discussion on fine points of certain shotgunning techniques, as we were taught by our fathers, and in some mild disagreement, too — both of us right in our own approaches — so it was a good-natured argument with some laughs going. Papa said that his father was a great wing shot but not so thorough and patient a teacher as mine, and that I was lucky in my environ, affording my father so much more time with us than his had. Then, a repeat of his oft-spoken "And you were lucky in competition with your older brother, and it would have been awfully good for me, too, if I'd had one to kick the hell out of me now and then, if I needed it or not, just to keep me in line. . . . My competition was a surrounding of sisters, and a brother just a kid when I was grown up and on my own."

Tillie chided him, asked if he was feeling sorry for himself. No, not at all, taking it very good-naturedly, then sensing the question in our minds, he told us of his father's suicide — in detail — of illness not too serious at his age; of a minor financial problem, magnified in his mind, and already solved had he taken the trouble to open his morning mail. But, he said, the basis of his father's dilemmas was domination, "by my mother, she had to rule everything, have it all her own way, and she was a bitch!"

Horrified, Tillie gasped, regained her breath, burst out, "Why, Ernest Hemingway, how dare you! How can you say that about your own mother?"

"Daughter, I can, and I do, because it's true . . . and I say it at the risk of losing your respect."

He went on: "True, it was a cowardly thing for my father to do, but then, if you don't live behind the eyes you can't expect to see all of the view. I know that part of his view, and I suppose he was mixing it up some . . . and you do such a thing only when you are tortured beyond endurance, like in war, from an incurable disease, or when you hasten a drowning because you can't swim all of the sea."

To appease her further, he put his arm around Tillie, said, "I'm sorry I burst out with it that way, should've kept it to myself. Tillie, but look . . . you know me now. Can you imagine me trying to learn, forced to be a musician? . . . I learned to play the first

six notes of 'My Country, 'Tis of Thee'. . . . Hmph! . . . And there went my liberty. See, I'd have done better at poetry."

"Papa, you devil, how can I give you hell?" Tillie said, and switched the subject to the great reading we were enjoying. From then on, if he was casually asked by the colonel or us, "How'd it go this morning, Papa?" he'd grin, say, "Oh, our book went great this morning, but yesterday. . . ."

Our book's progress slowed a bit in late November: a few days of warm, rainy weather; northern birds were down in numbers; the shooting "something to write about." One morning Papa and I threw a sack of decoys in the boat and Taylor worked afoot down one of the drainage canals within the loop of the creek, and met us at a little slough. We set the decoys, concealed ourselves and the boat in low willows, and waited but a short while for some business. In a short windy squall the rain turned to thick, blinding, wet snow, visibility maybe a hundred yards. Then out of nowhere came the rushing sound of old canvas being ripped apart. Any old slough rat will recognize that only one species of duck makes such a racket when they buzz your stool for a look: lesser scaup. They are absolutely fearless when they want to get down out of a storm. We almost had our hats taken, they came so low on the first pass; they circled into the murk and we got set. In action so fast that it's blurred in memory, we had time for but a glimpse of perhaps a hundred black specks boring straight at us. The van let loose and tumbled like bricks into our blocks, the followers coming so fast there wasn't room on the tiny open water; they zoomed up and we cut loose — three double guns, six shots. We shut our eyes and ducked our heads. Papa got one square in the belly; one hit my boot and half drowned me in icy water; one hung but an inch or two above the colonel's hat, in willow branches, and fell into his lap. Those six shots produced a baker's dozen and the dogs didn't know which way to start first. A half-hundred bewildered bluebills bobbed among our decoys, not twenty yards out, and took off when a voice out of the gloom said, "Sounds to me like a bunch of kids with more firecrackers than they know what to do with."

Chuck Atkinson, out hunting the canals with his dog, his coat bulging.

"You missed a good show, Chuck."

"The hell I did, a grandstand seat . . . how's your belly feel?"

"Okay . . . I guess . . . I haven't called foul yet, but he was awfully close."

Ours was a first experience of its kind. Up on the big marsh, the morning and evening shooting was also something to write about. We closed shop there and disposed of our blinds to avoid self-invitation by others snooping around the basin the following summer. Papa's friend Toby Bruce arrived December 1, Papa folded up his work, said that it was time to loaf and play before packing up for the departure. On Sunday, December 3, we had our second encounter with Stutter Man, in a surprise discovery in late afternoon. Papa and I did the lower half of the canoe run, not doing very well in a stiff wind, the day bright and sharp, Toby and Taylor waiting for us at pullout with the car. Up in the Chutes a ways we saw for the first time several flights of ducks, really carrying the mail, winging in over the long rocky ridge fingering down from the higher hills, its foot jutting out into the marsh. An odd behavior, but we figured it quickly; coming in from the open water of reservoirs some miles east, the ducks cut the corner instead of going around with the creek's meandering flow — to rest on its sheltered waters for the night. Papa was up front and he turned with the impish gleam in his eye: just beyond that ridge was

Stutter Man's old place, perhaps a hundred fifty yards to his backyard, a hundred feet lower in elevation.

I said, "Papa, you ornery bastard, what are we waiting for?"

"For two bastards to get up there," he said. "That's pass shooting, boy . . . deluxe stuff, and if we're not real careful we might rain down a little shot on his bridge . . . no turkeys there now, that's for true."

The colonel said he'd noticed that freak behavior, but kept it to himself, knowing damn well what we'd do. "Get up there," he said. "Take me across in your boat and I'll work the dog down on the flat, but I'll tell you this — you're going to have to shoot like you haven't shot before, this fall." He was so right — we missed four out of five until we realized just how great was their speed. The old place below was forlorn and deserted-looking, some wash hanging on a line; then suddenly old Stutter appeared from an old log outbuilding, flailing his arms like a windmill, yelling something we could not hear for the wind, and running pell-mell for the house.

"Jesus, kid, we'd better stay behind these rocks . . . the old muskrat may be going for a musket, and if he shoots like he talks we may come out short in the deal."

He came out on the porch with something in his hands, but we stayed low, downed one limit of ducks, watched them tumble slantingly for several hundred feet, bouncing off the flat like rubber balls. We let it quiet down then, and Papa stood up, yelled down his thanks for Stutter's courtesy — and that was the finish of the '39 fall shooting. It was hell getting up and down the rocky steepness of that ridge, but calling it a shooting banquet, under *those* conditions, is putting it mildly! Act Two for Stutter Man.

2.

The Family

Preparations for the '40 fall began early. As a result of his enthusiasm and curiosity for the saltwater fishing he'd never done, Taylor was invited by Papa to come to the Florida Keys, then over to Cuba to fish the Gulf Stream with him. The colonel took a leave of absence, left on a cloud in early April, and returned in mid-June. When he returned he was the color of copper, ten years the younger in manner and talk, and in his pocket was the money for a general hunting license and the small fee to accompany the application for the special antelope hunt permit.

"Papa's going great guns," he said. "Working like a beaver, and he hopes to make it for dove season the first of September. I told him that we'd get him fixed for that permit if we had to blackmail somebody."

I had heard something to that effect in our meager correspondence. In May I had sent Papa a hundred contact-size 4x5 photographs of the "El Sordo" country, some gorges for "the bridge" and other locale within easy driving distance. Bob Miles and I worked off and on a month at the job. If F.W.T.B.T. was to be made into a movie — an idiot would know that it would — damned if it wouldn't be made where part of it was written! The author responded with enthusiasm in his letter. In August Taylor sent the application to Boise for the permit drawing — the result was a telephone call from Papa.

"Damned if I don't believe your *governor* was blackmailed."

Right on the heels of his call came Toby Bruce escorting the Hemingway boys by train.

Their Papa's phoned instructions were simple: "Get them licensed, warm 'em up

on a few clay targets, and have us a dove feed on hand when we get there . . . I doubt that we'll make it on time, and if so, I've got work to do first."

He and Marty drove out in a new Buick convertible (how he got it so soon he wouldn't say), and arrived September 6. The work that he had a rush on was to check the final galley proofs of the book. He brought them to our shop for packaging on

Left: Gregory, at ten years, was as handy with a shotgun as most men.

The Hemingway "chips"—John (Bumby), Patrick (Mouse), and Gregory (Gigi).

September 10, then came through the door sideways in his elation at completing eighteen months of toil. The package was airmailed to Scribner's that morning.

"And damn," he said, "we were sorry to miss the fun . . . how many shells per dove, boys?"

"Awww, Papa, you're not supposed to ask us that!"

Seventeen-year-old Jack, called Bumby, was (and is) the real freshwater fisherman of the Hemingways — a dry-fly specialist to command the respect of our experts. Twelve-year-old Patrick and nine-year-old Gregory — "Mouse" and "Gigi" in that order — were the little shotgunners on their way up. Their reply to their father about their shooting speaks well enough of the strong ties; or maybe this is better: there were enough doves on ice for several feasts and the kids had held up their end.

Needless to say, there was a small celebration in Glamour House when the galleys were away, and I was asked if on the morrow I could take a few pictures "of my gang before we all get involved in things and Toby's here."

I said sure. He hadn't unpacked all his clothes yet, so he asked me what he should dig out to wear. I just looked at him and grinned.

"Sure." He laughed. "I'll get out my bulldogger's outfit."

My first casual glance at him that morning in '39 had brought to mind a big top-name rodeo performer whom I knew well from the Sun Valley shows. I told him so in our first talk, but said, "Who in hell ever saw a rodeo hand bareheaded, sleeves rolled up, and wearing a leather vest?"

"Nobody." He laughed. "You'd call him a damn phony."

So out came the identical outfit and the following morning I made the few shots over around the lagoon in the Inn village square. His publisher was asking for something special in conjunction with their promotion of the book. Right then there was not a damn thing for him to do that "looked like

Hemingway," as I frankly put it to him. Discussing it was the sort of situation that flustered Papa — yes, embarrassed him, and me. I said, "Oh, hell, Papa, you and Toby just lean there on your car and I'll make an informal shot or two of you talking or looking at something . . . pick out an object. . . ."

"We'll look at the bell in the Opera House belfry." He laughed. "And be thinking it's that time . . . about to toll five o'clock. How's that?"

"All right, be tasting the drink," I said. "So you won't look so damned stiff."

More by accident than anything else, I guess, he wiped the laugh off his face, and always at ease with his old friend Toby, he put one foot up on the log bordering the drive, a hand on his hip, the other arm leaning on the car. The finder showed it perfect for a second and I tripped the shutter. With a tongue-in-cheek attitude I said, "That'll do." He laughed, said, "That's the way we like it, short and snappy." I did the lab work myself, printed that casual shot "full" and in a tall "panel" of Papa alone, cropping-out Toby, who understood what I was after. Then the laughs.

"Damned if I don't look like I'm tasting a drink, Pappy . . . but I like it. It's a fine picture . . . know why? My hands, they don't look like *hams*. You can't call me the old bulldogger with them . . . hell, maybe I should've finished out as a 'cello player, after all."

So, my brief glimpse in the finder paid off: when Scribner's got the print they borrowed my "hands picture" negative, and I was told they printed it in a life-size panel for their book promotion. Indulge me at this writing to say that whenever Papa

Papa looks on as "Gigi" does some fancy calf-riding.

Hemingway comes to mind, that is my "image" of him way back when: forty-one years of age, savoring a monumental literary success. Foremost in his mind when my shutter clicked was the itch to get his rifle sighted in, sweating out the twenty-sixth of September when he hoped to get a buck antelope lined up in his sights. Instead he doffed his bulldogger clothes for shorts and a tennis racquet!

In his gun rack was a new Model 21 Winchester double barrel in 20-gauge, factory fitted with an extra set of barrels for long-range work. His promised gift to Marty on her birthday. So the interim was enough tennis to "go along" and stay in good with the amiable, social Father Daugherty — a good hand with a racquet himself — and lots of times at the shooting grounds. No finer double guns were ever built than the 21s, and hers was a good incentive for Marty; her successful efforts with it occasioned a memorable incident.

We made up a trap squad one day and locked the trap for straightaway targets — the "sleepers" that so often fool the experts because they look easy. Ernest did not care for traps, so he was the puller on the old pump handle cock-and-release; Marty, Tillie, Taylor, Stew Stewart, and myself on the line, moving through the full five positions, as usual. No one noticed a strange elderly couple watching from their car until we finished a round and the old man came out to ask if we intended another round — he hadn't shot trap in years, and would it be an imposition to shoot with us? Stew loaned him his gun and went to take over the pull stand; Ernest said no, he was enjoying the exercise. He delivered our targets perfectly on call, the old gent set a nice pace as lead-off man, and shot like a

38

house afire. In short, we had fun with the nice stranger and shot a second round. When finished he thanked us all like the perfect gentleman he was, and tipped the puller boy a silver dollar. There are no words to describe his chameleonlike expressions as the old man walked away.

Marty said, "Well, sonny, now that the trap season is about over, what'll you do then?"

"Well, let's see . . . three squads an hour is about average . . . three bucks, not bad wages . . . I'll put in my application for next summer now."

"I thought you were going to kiss the old man, Big E," Pop Mark cracked.

"I think I would have, Pop, if one of you had suddenly goosed me . . . first tip in my whole life. Pretty proud of this dollar."

On the hunt a good average pronghorn buck fell to the trusty Springfield — high on the west slopes of the Pahsimeroi. I didn't put in for the hunt (tied up with a special group of railroad guests), but at the time I had in mock-up the resort's first hunting brochure that Advertising had turned over to me for copywriting and illustrations. Chape, Ellis Chapin, a fishing guide who dabbled in photography, got a couple of good closeups of Papa and his antelope. He had told me that I could use any pictures that I thought suitable for such purpose. I showed Papa the one I preferred, and since paid-space advertising legally requires it, I had no choice but to ask him, of all people, to sign a model's release! I hear his laughter yet, but he said, "Hell, yes, Pappy, make it a blanket release until further notice. Might set me up with the John Powers Agency if times get rough."

"I'll do that, Papa, thanks very much. . . . Now since we're not allowed funds for model fees, we always make some sort of gesture, you know, and don't you rate pretty high?"

"You're damn right." He laughed. "Since I feel pretty cocky, no work to do

Gregory and Patrick Hemingway on their first duck hunt.

and back in the big dough again."

He was kidding but I was not. All the guides wore fine Pendleton shirts — the Inn store had given me several in return for promotional pictures and I had shirts to burn. I got a large one, black and white squares, and rolled it in a paper so that anyone would take it for a bottle. Papa was pleasantly surprised when I simply put it on the table beside him one day.

"Your compensation, *sir!*" I said. "Will Black and White do?"

"I'm being overpaid, *sir!*" He chuckled and picked it up, then the paper flew.

"Pappy, you bastard, you weren't joking . . . inch-square black-and-white checks."

He liked that fine shirt, wore it immediately and for a very long time.

On September 28 the Coopers arrived in midafternoon and were put up in the closed Lodge as usual. Coop came straight to my place with some hand-loaded big-game ammunition. He really had some awfully cute ways about him, made quite a cover-up to-do, talking our usual. I was leaving in a few days on another elk hunt in the Selway, taking a guest along. So, after so much palaver he eased into it, shyly:

"Now where you hidin' this fella Hemingway who I feel I know?"

Tillie had Papa on the phone, they talked a moment, and Coop said, "Thanks, Tillie gal, podnuh, see ya later, ah'll bet."

Though we knew the two would dovetail, we were intensely curious to witness this in-person meeting; but we had to be satisfied with a fitting description by Taylor: like two strange schoolboys sizing each other up, a line scratched in the dirt between them until "they got 'er done" in a

L. to R. Patrick Hemingway, T. Otto Bruce, Ernest Hemingway, Martha Gelhorn, Jack Hemingway and Gregory Hemingway with goose.

hurry. They seemed like old buddies when we arrived. The following day they got the measure they both looked for: we had a couple of hours over on the quail walk with the guns, and a round or two of skeet with Rocky, she who could shoot the pants off all of us at her specialty. Afterward came the incident that I'll never forget, and I remember it with warmth, and something else.

We pulled up in Coop's car in the square, for Papa to pick up his papers at the drugstore newsstand, and he said, "Will you run over the hill with us, you know?" For a second I didn't know, then caught on from his manner: he wanted to show Coop what Nin had had done for Gene's grave. She had remarried back in June — an assistant manager of one of the hotels — a quiet, nice chap named Winston McCrea. As soon as the ground was suitable in late spring, a local mason did a fine job of surrounding the two-plot space with a low stone wall, or fence, about a foot-high — solid, permanent as the mountains. The headstone is a large

natural granite boulder, its bronze tablet carrying Gene's name and the pertinent dates: 1905–1939. Beneath them is the last sentence of the eulogy that Ernest wrote and read:

HE HAS COME BACK TO THE HILLS THAT HE LOVED AND NOW HE WILL BE A PART OF THEM FOREVER.

Behind the stone she had planted two small lilac shrubs. Papa had been out with Nin to see it, was impressed with its

Toby Bruce and Ernest Hemingway in the new Hemingway convertible.

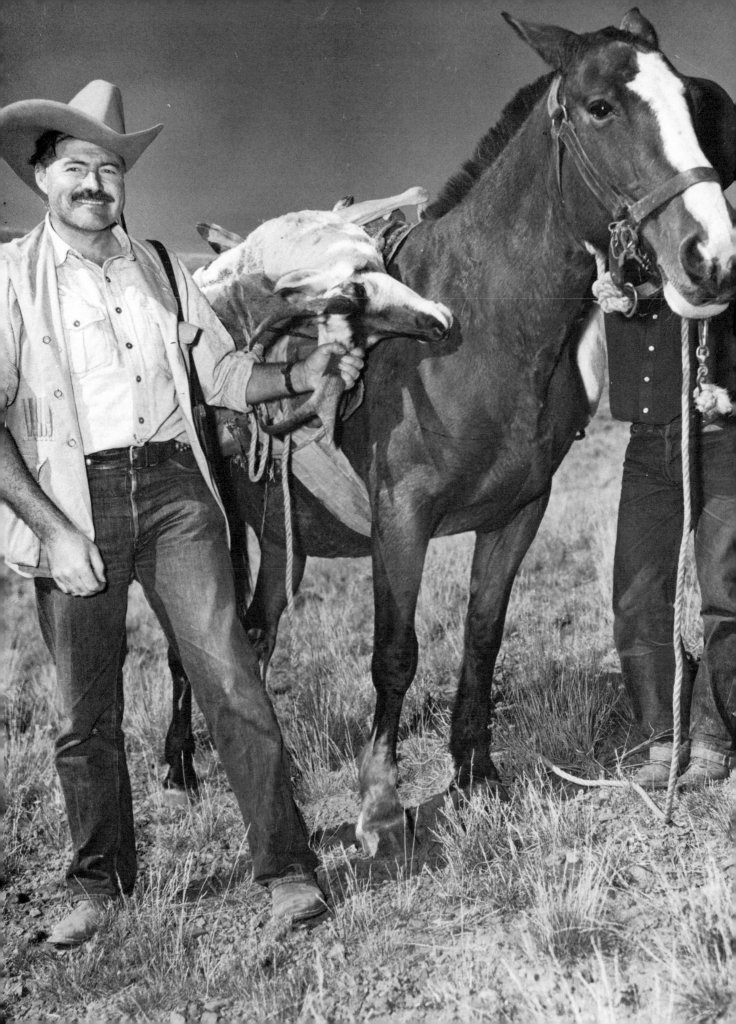

Far left: First big game in Idaho.

Left: Hunting partners Cooper and Hemingway, September, 1940.

Coop with a bobcat taken in the lava pits.

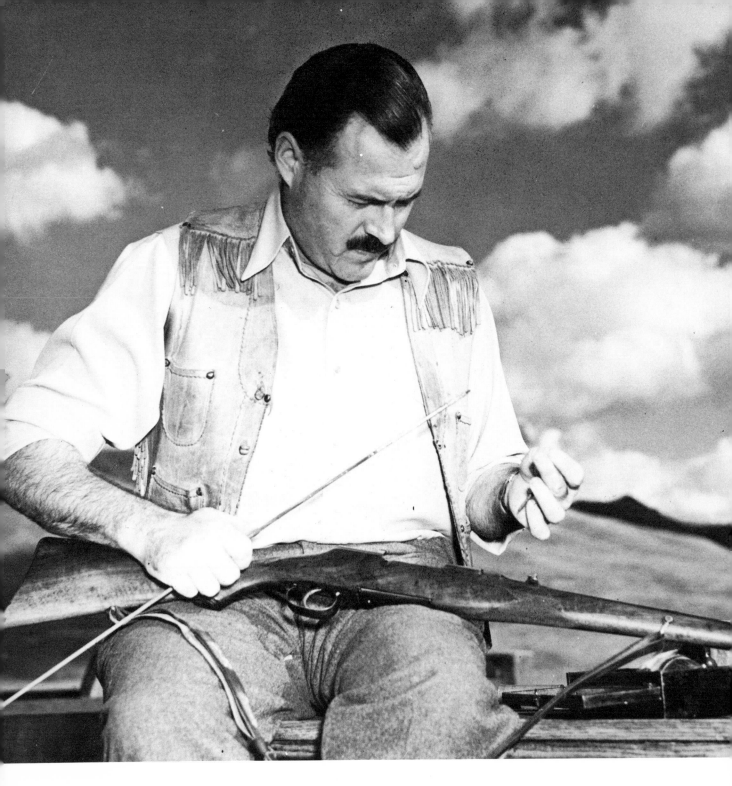

Cleaning the gun that brought home many dinners.

Overleaf:
The Great White Hunters Coop and Papa.

simplicity and expressed himself fully. Really, I was a bit surprised — I can't say why — that he spoke of it to Coop right off. Our visit was brief and simple.

"A hell of a guy," Papa said softly; Coop spoke in a soft affirmative, and that was all.

On October 3, our guest, whom we were nursing along as a fall regular, and I took off on our elk trip; I went on "company time" but otherwise on my own, and not for a trophy, but for good meat. I got it, with Bill Hamilton again at the helm, and we were back in five days. Again Ernest hoped to go, but was in correspondence and had phone calls about the book's publication. Of course, the meat was for the "pot" and I had to fight him in his insistence that he split my mild expense with me. I said in truth that I helped promote the thing for the fun of it, so he reluctantly backed off. In return for the good bourbon whiskey he had sent with me, Bill had again made a special effort to see that the "delicacies" came back with me in perfect shape.

No joke about those, they were the special treat while the quarters were curing. I've often mused that were it not for other things going on, Papa would have promoted their consumption around a campfire, like on safari.

The Coopers' stay was not a long one, about three weeks, but as Coop always said, "We got in the good licks, didn't we?" Rancher Tom Gooding hosted us on opening day of pheasants; something of a small army moved into his ample fields and those of his neighbors. Old Mr. Frees' area absorbed us nicely off and on, and that "general" put his army to use there in annihilating hundreds of the rabbit pests in the adjacent sage areas where they holed up during the day. The old man was right about the population rise; there were a couple of drives on his place that fall, and would have been more but for other factors. The duck season opened earlier that year, so some of that had to be tucked in with Coop. We had one good day in the blinds and one memorable one on the creek during his stay.

He shied a bit at the canoe trip, and it's a cinch that neither Taylor nor I could have got him into one, but you know who did. We made a leisurely fun day of it, took down another boat, and on the snaky upper stretch of the run with lots of shore growth for concealment, Taylor and I on the paddles, we drifted quietly side by side, the gunners taking turns on the rises. It was more fun watching the two big kids at their fun, both of them more than willing to spell us, but not arguing about it. We had both dogs along, did a little business in our "bluebill" slough, and loafed over lunch on Picture Bridge — breaking it with a sortie or two on foot for snipe. They were the first that Coop ever shot "at" and let me say for the record that the old easygoing cowboy's vocabulary could match a Seventh Cavalry trooper's any day — when the going was rough. I remember no day in many years when he had more fun.

Up to then, the only press release on Ernest was the antelope hunt. This, more than anything else, not to "push" the publicity on him (we'd get that anyway in the press notices on the book, and another deal); don't make a big thing of it was the dictum. Pictures had been made only on a couple of Trail Creek parties, more or less for fun. I had a camera along that day, used it casually around the bridge — no objections at all, the opposite, in fact — then, waiting for the later flight movement we just sat around talking on the log rail of the bridge. I had my boots off, having shipped a little water, and suddenly Papa picked up several snipe, kidding Coop about them. Of course he was inviting me to take a picture of the three of them, the dogs included. I popped one, it looked awfully good as a casual, so I made another and "directed" that one. That did it, so we horsed around at making a number, just for kicks. We were home early and I brought proof prints to the dinner table late that night. They were all personal hits, but that one with Papa holding the snipe in his hand, Coop in the middle, Taylor kneeling with his gun for a staff, was "my" picture, and I knew what to do with it. The Hannagan man, a genial, laughing Irishman, kicked it off in a release. Probably long forgotten now, it was syndicated, the clipping returns came in by the sackful, a record for a long

time.

All of which is to say that's how it was with Papa Hemingway — easy, casual, no fuss about it, and rewarding. And let us not forget to place most of the credit with the environs: a warm, golden, shirt-sleeves day, the soft murmur of water, contented canine companions — a party of *basically* atavistic primitives.

On October 22 the airmail brought a box of the first edition of *For Whom the Bell Tolls* — about a dozen copies, all of which were pegged for certain people about the premises and elsewhere. By then that "no work to do" business was a laugh — an elated one. Mr. Author needed a full-time F.W.T.B.T. secretary and a private switchboard to handle the phone calls, and the daily mails swamped a favorite bellboy. As expected, Hollywood was hot on the scent for film rights — one notable producer-director had already visited Sun Valley and there had been talks, but no deal. Then from Hollywood came the man who got it — the head of the story department of the Myron Selznick Agency. He was Don Friede, who Papa said was the one before he came — a long-standing obligation. Friede was once an editor for an early publisher, and helpful in the struggling days. Don, a quiet, all-business sort, spent two days in camp, practically all of it poring over the book. We wondered how he absorbed it so fast. Afterward there was a phone call to Papa's lawyer, the deal was settled, and Don took the bus for the afternoon train.

Prior to that was an amusing incident relevant to the record price the story brought. It was a drizzly day spent in Glamour House on reviews, columns, and God knew what all — some drinking too, but not excessive, tempered with lunch sent over from the Inn. This in a period of about six hours, then suddenly Papa jumped up from a heap of papers and periodicals, said, "Let's go shoot some targets." A damn good idea — fresh air was a must. Not a soul on the grounds but Stew Stewart locking up the

skeet layout. Okay, we'd shoot the unwanted skeet because? . . . How he did it, I don't know, but Papa broke twenty-four out of twenty-five.

In the midst came a phone call from Hollywood. There was some cursing. Then on the porch he said to Stew and me, "Goddamn, that was big dough I was talking to, shouldn't have been so short with 'em, I guess . . . but Christ! I wish they wouldn't call during our working hours."

It was one of several calls from Twentieth Century-Fox, but Paramount got the story.

Early in November the long-coming divorce from Pauline materialized. Little comment here, other than Papa often saying that they were friends with an under-standing, and they always would be. I remember but a single change of pace at the time: a sober, nontalkative ride home from a pheasant hunt. There were just we two in his car, so I know that it was real.

Also early that month came a good break. Papa's friend from the Spanish Civil War days, photographer Robert Capa, came out on a story for *Life* magazine, an arrangement no doubt with the Hemingway finger behind it. Intended as a story documenting the book and its eventual filming, it also covered the goings-on at Sun Valley. It came out in the January 6, 1941, issue, after the November Hemingway-Gellhorn wedding, so Capa's picture story was shot with that in mind, too.

The little Hungarian, short, dark, beetle-browed and moody, eternally dangling cigarette squinting his eyes, well, Capa was different; what he did in his field had size to it. He shot his 35mm cameras like miniature rapid-fire guns, and put some meaty human-interest stuff on film. We took him down the creek in the canoe, scared hell out of him a time or two, but you didn't scare him long — he had nerve, plenty. One segment of his piece concerned our habitual hunting on a thousand-acre farm in the fringe area west of Shoshone — fantastically

good pheasant cover on most of it. The little farmer's name we could not pronounce — about a foot long on his mailbox; he was Balkanese — so Papa simply called him John Myers. John had thirteen children in stairsteps up from a nursing infant; a house so small that you wondered how they were stacked for sleeping; they ate in relays.

Duck hunting at Silver Creek.

A successful antelope hunt in the fall of 1941.

Concerned as they were with the business of eking out a living on the run-down place, the Hemingway name meant not a damn thing to them. Needless to say, we seldom took a bird home from John's farm, for a butchered elephant carcass could have been ditched about the clutter of buildings. John shot with us, and when our party had

enough guns, one of his youngsters would mount a horse and follow to carry the birds. I've seen the feathered load outweigh the boy more than once. One cold fruitful day we came in, Mrs. Myers cooked a noon meal, and Capa had a time of it getting his angles in the cramped house. We headed out again and finished up in midafternoon.

Then, before leaving, we went to work in the yard on a gallon jug of claret.

For a few days Papa had been trying to figure a graceful way to get John's pickup truck back in the running. It was sick with clutch and transmission trouble, there was daily milk to get to town, for which John had to depend upon a neighbor. Papa asked me if I thought it was worth fixing up, and I said, yes, and it was. Suddenly we "had to go" behind the barn: how much cash did I have in my pocket? Between us there was enough. When we left, Papa slipped the half-full jug on the truck's seat, told John to have it towed into town by his neighbor and get it fixed — we'd see him in a few days. The jug was corked with familiar green paper. The fall party was about to break up so we did not see John again for a year. A straight statement to Capa, who'd caught on: "Report that in your story and I'll wring your neck."

He smiled with it and Capa kept his word, but. . . .

There was one incident in which he didn't.

When we went behind the barn that day, Papa took his gun along, for there was a weed patch down a short slope that often produced pheasants. My weapon was my gun-stocked movie camera, and I hadn't turned a wheel with it. We finished the monetary thing and Papa said it just might be our luck to walk out there and do some business for both of us. I fell in behind him, and damned if a cock pheasant didn't roar out, a sharp-angle shot that Papa missed with his under barrel, though he winged the cock with his upper. The bird recovered from his bouncing fall, but gave Papa time to slip in reloads before he took off like a quarter horse. He ground-sluiced him for the count and I was able to get into position to grind off film on that much of it. My old print of the film shows Papa walking into the camera, the wings flopping; he drops the bird, picks it up and comes on (pretty good actor, too).

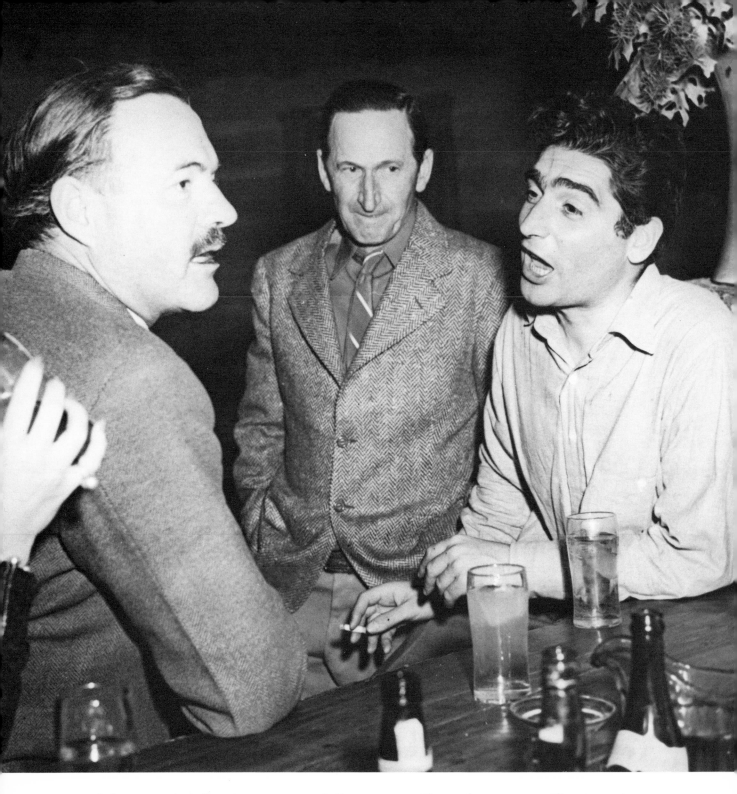

Life *magazine's Robert Capa arguing with Papa.*

The cock was a magnificent specimen, in his prime, and I made a couple of kodachromes for myself with my Leica. Papa said, "This is about the heaviest pheasant I've ever hefted . . . boy, isn't he a beauty!"

Here was the "lead" picture for the Idaho part of Capa's story; I said so, and Papa agreed, yelled out in the voice you heard a mile, and Capa came on the double. Whenever I look at its full-page spread in my file copy of *Life*, I think to myself: This is as fine, and typical of Papa Hemingway in that era, as any picture I know. Then I smile to myself, too. The caption reads: "Photographer Capa reports that Dead-shot Hemingway, in ten days of hunting, never missed a bird." The caption angered him plenty.

His beef was that in view of *Life*'s great circulation, countless gunners would laugh up their sleeves, knowing full well that the best wing shots do well in averaging 60 percent. Fine shot that he was, Papa's average was in the top bracket, his misses in proportion. In this, he was scrupulously honest, and had told Capa of such averages. In a letter to Taylor and me he said that when he saw Capa again he'd have a boot poised for him — sidewise, so it would lift him!

Another incident during Capa's visit was a classic, the occasion a prewedding, going-away party at Trail Creek cabin. Marty's mother was out from St. Louis, a gracious lady whom Papa called a rare jewel. As he put it, his party was for her, Capa, "and everybody who's made everything so good for us this short fall." All males put on their party-going rigs and wore ties! Chape and I took a camera between us and used it sparingly, for fun. The cabin bar in those days was very small and boxed-in, entered via the kitchen. The drinking was mild all around, and of course Papa perched himself on a stool and remained there until the dinner gong. With his jacket pockets full of flashbulbs (the big ones that were all we had then) Capa fired away at his favorite human subject, then finally got up on a stool behind the bar, for some bizarre angles, I guess. Every shot that he fired showed Papa with a drink in his hand or on the way up — and at it. Papa told him three times to get the hell down off that stool — "What're you tryin' to do, portray me as a rummy?"

Capa let up on him for a bit, but stayed

up there, then started sneaking a few shots when his subject's eyes were turned. He had a spring-loaded ejector in his flashgun and accidentally kicked out a spent bulb — smoking hot — that would have burst on the bar right in front of Papa but he caught it in both hands and flipped it right back, catching Capa square between the eyes! The whole maneuver happened so fast you could hardly follow it. Capa said not a word, got down with the sullen look of injured pride, while Papa's "Now, goddamnit, am I a friend or just a son of a bitch of a target to you?" injured him further. He came out into the room, laid his camera down carefully, then the torrent broke.

He tore off his loosened tie, flung his jacket in a corner, and lit into Papa like he was ready to kill him. There were probably thirty of us present, and I doubt if there was a closed mouth among us. His tirade was half-English, half something else, and for a bit we wondered if he was about to get tossed outside in the creek just off the front porch. Papa told the barkeep to fix his madman friend a drink and put a little castor oil in it at the instant my flashbulb went off, catching the scene. I just couldn't resist it, I guess. Anyway, the flash broke the tension, Papa commenced to laugh, and slowly Capa turned on the sheepish grin, wound the film in his camera back into its cartridge, and gave it to Papa who put it in his pocket — still laughing. At the table, Capa went noble. He picked up his empty camera and a fat candle in a wrought-iron holder and made a picture of the about-to-be-weds. The date was November 14.

The boys had departed by train — to catch up on their schooling — and for reasons of their own, the wedding was not to be in Sun Valley, "just somewhere down the line on our way home." Finally, Papa hit upon Cheyenne as the place, said they would tie the knot simply — "give the string to a Justice of the Peace . . . we like peace and justice, don't we?"

While the packing was in progress, Marty said, "By all the dusty old standards, wouldn't it be nice if we had a wedding picture . . . wonder who'd make one for us, just a casual something?"

They were casual, all right, but good — profile shots using only natural light on the sun deck, one with Ernest (Marty's only address for him) pointing at an imaginary something toward the afternoon sun. We ran off prints in a hurry, and agreed on that one as the best.

"I'll bet that I can plant this as a full page in *Harper's Bazaar*," Marty said. "The more I look at it the better I like it."

"Now if Pappy and I had our way we'd plant it in *Field and Stream* . . . more in keeping with the life we live out here . . . but say, I look like I'm pointing to the dark future."

Once again the bulk of the gear and books was stored with us; the Hemingway confidence said there would be another fall free of war involvement. I, the pessimist, did not go along with him, but in standing his ground he'd merely grin, say, "You'll see, kid . . . of course, I could be wrong." Tillie and I were flattered, and touched, by both Marty and Ernest urging us to go with them — to Cheyenne, to Omaha, Denver, anywhere along the line as we saw fit — or, "Hell, come to Key West with us, and on over to the new place in Cuba." We don't fully recall why we didn't take him up and have always regretted it. Their departure was on November 19.

On November 21, a Cheyenne justice of the peace did the honors, and on the twenty-second Tillie and I got a telegram from there:

WE HOPE THAT WE CAN LIVE UP TO OUR WEDDING PICTURES AND ALSO TO BE AS GOOD A PAIR AS YOU TWO.

When she read it, my seldom-swearing Tillie did say, "Damnit, why didn't we go with them, at least that far?"

On December 9 came this telegram from New York:

PICTURE US TWO ERNEST POINTING DARK FUTURE WITH RIGHT HAND TAKEN BY HARPER'S FULL PAGE SPREAD EXCLUSIVE WITH BYLINE YOURS STOP PLEASE DON'T GIVE TO ANYONE ELSE HAVE ARRANGED WITH LIFE NOT TO USE STOP EVERYTHING FINE HERE CLOSELY RESEMBLING LIFE IN RUNAWAY ELEVATOR STOP AM OFF TO BURMA ROAD SOONS POSSIBLE STOP ALL THIS AND HEAVEN TOO LOVE TO THE GANG. MARTY.

No surprise at all in the Burma Road announcement; that had been a sharp burr under the Hemingway blanket most of the fall. Marty angled hard to get the *Collier's* assignment to cover the China-Burma Road theater that was the headline news on that side of the world. Someone else got it, then was decided against, and Marty landed it.

"Well, all right, but by God, she can't go alone . . . it's too rough a trip, especially for a woman, and I won't allow it, and I'll wangle some sort of deal as an escort."

(He did, with the newly organized *PM* magazine headed by Ralph Ingersoll.)

With us it was an out-in-the-open bitch about the whole thing, and Marty was assailed from all sides. Tillie's arguments against her going were friendly intervention, and accepted as such. Marty simply told her that she wanted that assignment "more than anything in the world."

The informative telegram was followed shortly by a note from Papa; said he was carrying around a six-figure check in his pocket and guessed he'd better deposit it before the digits were worn off. Near Christmas we wracked our heads to figure out some cute tokens as gifts and good luck for the coming Asiatic trip. We had gone on the deer hunt — Taylor, Chape, and I — a successful one netting us three record-book heads that adorned the big Lodge lounge fireplace for many years. With our gifts we sent pictures to Papa, who expressed his delight with our success — as pleased as if he'd been along: "We're going to have to go into the hills together some time."

There were some nice gifts for us, Tillie's a thing that she wore for a long time afterward, and the affectionate note with them was signed "With much love, always. Gellstein and Hemhouse."

Youngest son Gigi sizes up his father's game.

3.

"That Unshakable Hangover"

This chapter's quote comes from that fall; but the insight behind it was gained much earlier — in the Far East, the China-Burma theater. There were complications in their preparations during the winter, and it was early spring before they got under way. Delayed a few days in San Francisco, Papa called us from there one night. In contrast to his beefing back in the fall, he was quite airy about the Far East trip, but in the conversation he said that they'd had so many innoculations, so much needlejabbing into their anatomies — Marty was still dragging with aftereffects — that he guessed they were both eligible for the Purple Heart.

"I hear San Francisco is lousy with needle artists and I'm gonna find me a good one and have mine tattooed on my ass!"

It was good, however, to hear him so cheerful; they would let us know when they set foot on home soil again — and by God, it had better be damn well ahead of fall! They flew the Pacific and we got word from Havana in July that they'd made it. Taylor had fished the Florida Keys that spring and had seen Papa briefly when they left for Asia; so he had the fall plan and acted upon it.

In August he sent Papa's application in for another antelope permit, and damned if the Big H wasn't lucky again! Taylor drew one, I missed — and was disappointed because I had a free time spot around the date. The three boys again arrived — by train — ahead of the dove season. Toby Bruce took factory delivery of a Lincoln Continental convertible and drove it out to Idaho for Papa, arriving September 6. It was a beautiful car — one of the all-time classics of design — a dreamily comfortable thing to drive; to be sure, it was a prestige car, but it

Papa and Taylor ("The Colonel") Williams on an antelope hunt.

sure as hell was not for Idaho "safari" use! It was September 14 when its owner and his equally tired bride arrived. Toby met their train in Shoshone.

Papa decided to try the accommodations at the Inn this time. Their quarters were on the second floor of the wing jutting out into

Marty's honesty confessed that she'd never have made it without Ernest. She said she was never so glad to see anything in her life as the sight of the Golden Gate Bridge on their return flight.

This time Papa flatly declared that he'd swept his docket clean of work, and would answer only the most important mail. "We'd better make this a good fall, if we can," he said. "I see an interruption, not too far off." The invigorating mountain air banished their weariness quickly; there was an active season ahead, as the booking showed, and the fun started at once — with the elegant sage green Lincoln, its top folded down, and bulging with seven of us.

The general had to inspect the Silver Creek theater right off and took the wheel himself for the jaunt. Everything went fine until the country road around the creek run. At a midway place called the Point-of-Rocks there was a mudhole — a seeping spring — that the general knew like the palm of his hand. But somehow he missed the right wheel ruts and promptly bogged her down, square in the middle of it. We pushed and heaved to no avail. Toby tried to drive it out, I tried. We didn't know what automobile history now concedes: the original Continentals were notoriously underpowered, but we got the hunch then. We saw a Sabbath-working farmer plowing a field with a team and got him to pull us out.

"Why, this 3-G son of a bitch can't pull itself over a fence post the size of my arm."

Translate 3-G, please, General.

"Just a few thousand bucks worth of gutless green giant, that's what, but ain't she pretty though, mud dripping off her belly like an underslung sow!"

The pretty sow took us on a trip up into the Bitteroot Mountain country of western Montana. Taylor had several elk hunts booked in the Selway and had to arrange with packers to "spread them out" in the area. We only mentioned it, and Papa said it was the perfect time for him to see the country he'd missed twice, keying himself

the Village Square. Plainly utilitarian, they were far handier to all services. The trip to the Asian war was a harrowing thing, an experience, a circus — and revealing! Since I vowed to record only personal experiences herein, I'll just say that it was great listening, spread over the fall, and that up, admittedly. There were four of us: Papa, Taylor, "Big A" Wood — a big, shuffling guide with a sense of humor far ahead of his gait — and myself, and we picked up Bill Hamilton on the way. As we were winding up the Trail Creek Summit road, which that fall got the first improvement on its lower half in sixty years, a rolling rock knocked a hole in the exhaust pipe. We yelled ourselves hoarse for forty miles to Challis and a mechanic with a welding torch for repairs.

While in the Bitteroot country we went on up to Lolo, Montana, and west over the historic Lewis and Clark Trail — then merely a crooked little old wagon road down the Lochsa River in Idaho — to our old base camp. With our sleeping bags we roughed it overnight, the smells of the big wild in our nostrils, of steaks broiled over an open fire, on a wire grill that we bought on the way. In the morning, sniffing the good bacon and coffee boiling, Papa said that of the many places he'd seen, the big down-timber, rough and rolling Selway was as typical an example of a man sensing his rightful place in nature's scheme of things as you'd find. That was as close to that sort of thing as we ever got, but it was a glimpse of the man Ernest Hemingway, stripped down to the essentials, that left an indelible impression on me.

I said little on that pleasant trip about him elking with us that fall, but knowing that I was itching to twist his arm until I near broke it, his remark to the effect was: "We'll see what the toll on the antelope hunt is, Pappy . . . damn, I wish that you had drawn a permit too, I feel like a cheater."

A little incident when we got back almost tipped him into going with me farther south in the Selway. He called it a good-luck omen, and maybe it was. A cook in the Inn kitchen had a little 6.5-caliber Mannlicher-Schoenauer carbine — identical to his except for double-set hair triggers. Too short-range for our Western hunting,

the rifle was, and is, a classic in design, workmanship, and general appeal. I had tried to buy the gun just as a pride-of-possession thing, but the cook wouldn't sell. Then, quitting the Valley for somewhere else, he put it up for raffle — tickets a dollar each. One of the Ram waiters told us about it at dinner, said there were a half-dozen tickets left. Fairly well steeped in the juice of the grape we dug in our pockets and came up with about that much between us. Sure, hell yes, close the raffle now! Within minutes the cook "shook 'em up" and a waitress reached into his tall cap and pulled out ticket number 27.

"Now, we're partners in something of material value, Chief . . . what in hell will we do with it?"

"Set it in the rack and admire it," I said. "Something to brag about to our jealous friends, huh?"

And so we did — because the rack had to be full, "so that we look well armed in season, prepared for any emergency."

The antelope hunt turned out to be quite an event, worthy of being written up by Papa Hemingway "for dough" years later in a popular man's magazine. But now the prelude of the trip seems more important, as Hemingway history.

Impressed with Taylor's and my success with our light .257 rifles, Papa itched to try the caliber on an antelope. We did our best to focus the 'scope on my converted Springfield — the action he naturally preferred — but his eye would not take it, so he switched to Taylor's Winchester and its iron sights; Taylor used my gun. I went along as cameraman, hoping to augment the good movie footage that I'd made in the summer with telephoto lenses. Ours was a sizable party; there were two other guest hunters guided by Jack Redden, and Papa took the boys, Bumby to fish the Pahsimeroi River, the youngsters for the ride. We set up camp in an old bunkhouse-cookshack combination on Ray Hamilton's ranch well up in the valley; Sun Valley sent a cook with us, the best in grub. Bill Hamilton, who had ridden the slopes on the valley's west side, reported ample average heads, one buck of record-book size, another a true freak. The pronghorns' headgear is unique in the animal world — distinctly American — and this fellow had horns that curved sharply forward, out over his brow, in profile resembling an eyeshade, instead of the majestic upward-flaring straightness. Papa said he'd go after him — he was no good for seed — and one of the hunters suggested they flip a coin for him. Taylor put his foot down, told all his guests to go for the best — he'd take the freak if we could find him on the morrow.

It was settled over a fine steak supper in the smoky lantern-lit bunkhouse, with Ray's ranch hand joining us, and heavily hitting the jug of good red wine. We knew him only as Wild Bill — a big, jovial, strapping man, Papa's counterpart in build, in his mid-twenties, and rarin' for fun, which he knew where to find. At the head of the forty-mile-long valley there was feverish mining activity at a place called Patterson — a mushroom camp, wild and woolly, in pursuit of the vital metal tungsten. Wild Bill was bent on going to Patterson, and Ray warned us to stay away from the place at night — offshift miners had little to do but drink and fight. But something different was a fascinating lure, so Papa, Jack Redden, and myself ignored the warning and about nine o'clock went out with Wild William. I drove my own car (thank God) and Ray warned Papa not to wear his big hat, and to pull his pants legs over his boots, not tuck them in. That he did, but wore the hat. Ray's reasoning was sound: he said that a drunken miner might take big Ernie for one, too, and tell him that he was a better one — what then? Papa said, "I'll agree with him, Ray, and get the hell out of his way, if it's out in the street even, with lots of room."

Street, hell! It was a dusty lane of dozed-off sagebrush, dimly lighted with naked electric lamps hanging over the void, bordered by eateries and saloons — all mere thrown-together shacks. The bedlam emitting from them was deafening, the air the kind that you could grab in handfuls. We parked in a dark vacant lot beside one of the saloons that Wild Bill recommended in fuzzy-voiced enthusiasm. Crowded to capacity, its mob was friendly, yelling out "Hi, Bill," on all sides. The whiskey was good and the barkeeps poured with their eyes shut. More was spilled by jostling than was drunk of the single round we had, edging away from the raw wet planks of the wall-to-wall bar. Bill's reason for choosing the place was obvious: to tangle with a man — as big as any I ever saw — mean-looking pig eyes slitting hate at Bill who, in his state, tried to return it, doing a fair job. Weaving like his boots were nailed to the floor, he'd have tackled the giant had Papa not edged his way between them. He hissed to us, "We'd better get the hell outa here, there's a few guys taking this in, maybe friends of the big one, and there'll be hell to pay if either of these two makes a move."

But the big man had his plan. He edged away, then headed for the door, Bill trying to follow him, Papa holding him back with a body block. We waited some time, things looked normal, and I headed out, said I'd start my car. Good. Nothing in sight, so I turned my lights on dim, left the doors open, and went back onto the flimsy plank porch to see our bunch talking outside with some "good guys," obviously. I nodded that the coast seemed clear, and the dusty street was empty in all directions. Suddenly a young man about my size appeared, carrying a battered tin suitcase, heading straight our way — a drifter, no doubt, looking for a bunk tonight, a job tomorrow. Before any of us could stop him, Wild Bill lurched down the steps, hauled back a long right and walloped the slender man on the side of his head, sitting his behind in a cloud of dust. Weaving over him, Wild Bill said he was not

the son of a bitch he was looking for, mumbled an apology, and just started to help the man up when the one he was looking for lurched out from the shadows of my car, cocked and ready. His right hit Bill high on the head, and Bill got in a lick and went to his knees, the big man staggering back against my car. He recovered quickly and moved in, a long leg and a huge hobnailed boot primed for the business. In a swift leap off the porch Papa was between them. His right hauled back and·in a blur landed on the side of the man's face, whacking like a lath on a barn door. His towering target folded down like an accordion, his lolling head barely missing my bumper. Shaking in our boots, Jack and I left the porch in jumps, a mob boiling out the door behind us. Papa pulled the innocent to his feet, who asked who and why. His reply was: "Don't wait to ask the cooled one. Get going, and thanks for having that suitcase for him to kick outa the way first."

He and Jack heaved the half-out Bill into the car, and we were off in a cloud of frantic dust, nobody saying a word, but hanging on as I drove out of that mess like I'd never driven before. Safely out, with no lights trailing us, Papa leaned forward in the dash lamp glow to seek the answer to my question: "How's the hand, Papa, it sounded bad to me, that crack . . . you're supposed to shoot with it tomorrow."

He grinned up at me, a still-spooked look in his eye.

"Okay, I guess, stings a bit, but I saved it with my grips."

He reached into his jacket pocket and came up with a half-dozen of our hot hand-loaded .257 cartridges, saying, "How's our boy Bill, Jack?"

Bill mumbled something to Jack's, "All right, I think, a skinned knuckle or two, some blood."

"Sure, he connected with the big guy's collarbone . . . in the morning his right will look like a green cantaloupe — with fingers. Jesus, I'm lucky the biggest man in a long time was boozed up, and I never saw such boots in my whole life."

He was right about that, and a man's head might have been pulped that night if fast-thinking Papa Hemingway hadn't moved like a streak of human lightning. We got Bill into bed, sneaked quietly in ourselves, and in the morning it was covered up by Papa joking that someone bet Bill he couldn't put his fist through a ply-paneled door — hit the frame, instead. "Come on, kid, I'll saddle your horse for you."

At ten o'clock, with Papa and the boys far off on a ridge holding the freak buck's attention, the colonel stalked afoot to a low ridge and nailed him clean with a single shot at a long three hundred yards. When Papa rode down, he said, "Great shooting with a strange rifle once more, Colonel . . . it's a fine little cartridge, good for antelope, good for fisticuffs — minus the Queensbury rules."

There was nothing wrong with the big-bodied buck that we could determine in dressing him out — as the colonel said, nature just saw fit to equip him with a fancy hat — and he was alone when shot, an outcast to the apparently finicky antelope ladies.

We fanned out on our horses then and searched hard for the big buck Bill had reported. We passed up some ordinary heads and ate our lunch on the high backbone of the Pahsimeroi Mountains as they dipped off to the Salmon far below to the north, shining brightly in the warm September sun. Our glasses eventually picked up a small band headed by a good average buck and the long stalk down began,

the boys following slowly, well behind. We worked it well, got into position behind a low and rocky ridge that afforded concealment. A nod from Papa said for me to belly up, take a look, and use my judgment on trying for some telephoto footage. It was there, all right, the band about two hundred yards off, grazing along quietly, slightly below me on a long flat. Then I almost loused up the whole deal by forgetting that my long lens barrel was a brightly polished raw metal. It surely flashed a sun reflection and the band took off in a buff-colored streak, due broadside to me, down toward a long fingering ridge that, if reached, it was good-bye, Mr. Buck. I frantically waved for Papa to come on the double; he did, cursing a blue streak, ran on by me twenty yards, skidded to a stop, raised his rifle, and in a barely perceptible pause in lineup, let off his single shot. The buck, as usual in the midst of the does and fawns, just disappeared as the rest went over the ridge. I silently cursed myself, but breathed a sigh of relief as Papa stood there, not believing it himself.

"How far would you say, Pappy?"

"Pretty close to three hundred," I said. "And for a minute I thought there would be no shot to ask about . . . sorry, Papa. . . ."

"What spooked 'em, kid? . . . It was a perfect setup."

I spoke of my theory, and he said, "Sure, that had to be it, I didn't hear your camera running. . . . Well, good! . . . I've made fair shots in my time but this ranks them all . . . what a hell of a cartridge, a hell of a rifle."

"The understatement of your life," I said. "You still haven't got your wind back."

The buck was in perfect shape as it hadn't run far enough to heat up for meat-tainting. It was hit at shoulder point at an even two hundred seventy-five yards, carefully stepped off on the easy terrain and double-checked with my range finder. Accuracy-stickler Papa was in charge of that, modestly shy about it, but happy as a kid at

Stalking a buck in the Pahsimeroi Valley.

the luck element coupled with the know-how of the born hunter.

The man who was my partner on the elk hunt got the big head — a fine trophy animal — and all permits were filled. Needless to say, there was no Patterson proposal for the night following that successful day, and his antelope was the last big game that Papa Hemingway collected on his home continent.

Ten years later he wrote it up for *True* magazine, a piece entitled "The Shot," published in the July, 1951, issue. In its leading paragraphs he said of his good friend Taylor Williams: ". . . who can kill you dead with a borrowed rifle at three hundred yards!" It was typical of Papa not to mention it to the colonel, who had fished the Gulf Stream with him but a short while before the story appeared; instead he sent us copies of the magazine. I sat right down and wrote him for both of us, kidding him that he had left out the reason that he made that remarkable shot with a slightly sore hand. His reply made no mention of that, but it said, "I wish, Pappy, that it were so we could come out to Idaho this fall and spend the dough that I got for the piece with you guys."

Again luck smiled on me in the Selway. I returned with a fine meat animal on October 9 and drove in shortly after the Gary Coopers. There was a fresh liver feed that night, when Papa had us all in stitches with a rundown of high points from their Oriental trip; and as a storyteller Marty could match him any day. We got the serious side of it, too, when the Hemingway crystal ball flatly said that our entry into the world conflict would come in the Pacific.

"We'll probably get it for a Christmas present," said he. "Or maybe wake up New Year's morning with an unshakable hangover."

There loomed the ominous fact that our

Howard Hawks,
Marty Hemingway,
and Gary Cooper.

Coop and Marty
Hemingway cutting
a rug at the cabin.

The family and a bag of pheasants.

Coop, Papa, and Taylor Williams, chief hunting and fishing guide.

relations with Japan had gone from bad to worse when, that summer, President Roosevelt had frozen Japanese assets, which effectually cut off her oil supply. That is what would eventually embroil us, Papa Hemingway predicted. So, to repeat him, we made it as good a fall as we could — and it was a great one, in which the general had

Taylor and Barbara Stanwyck — then Mr. and Mrs. and both riding high on their careers. From Washington, D.C., and the White House, came busy Lend-Lease administrator Averell Harriman and his younger daughter Kathleen; and the John Boettigers — President Roosevelt's daughter Anna and her husband. It was more for true than joke that Papa, before this group arrived, kidded about going "on a binge with Mrs. Benge." Mrs. B. had a little shop in Ketchum, in which she designed and turned out leather jackets, coats, and vests of real class and of the finest chamois, antelope, and kid skins — any colors. A specialty of hers was pullover hunting shirts. There was no bigger sucker for fine leather stuff than Papa Hemingway. So he went all out, had several things made, including a white capeskin hunting shirt. "Going Hollywood," he said. "Don't you think I'm as handsome as Plainsman Hickok Cooper in this fancy shirt?" Well, he was pretty handsome, at that; at least his coloring was a striking contrast to the neat white party rig. Anyone would know there would be plenty of parties with that group in camp.

It was Mr. Harriman's first fall visit to the resort in his charge. His time was short, and he didn't intend to hunt. He came to the shop one morning when I was there alone, honing down a welded ejector rod that had snapped in Papa's Browning. I saw lots of him when he came, but seldom did he visit the shop, so I had a hunch that he was wondering why the Hemingway quarters were in the Inn that fall. The two had never met. I went on honing while he asked about the hunting, and directly I was asked where in the Inn Mr. Hemingway lived. I pointed out his windows in the wing not sixty feet from us, where Papa sat typing at a little table — the broken gun kept us in that morning and I was trying to get it ready for an afternoon shoot. In his pleasantly blunt way, Mr. Averell grinned, said, "See that you do, looks to me like you might." I

some notable additions to his little army of gunners.

Following the Coopers from Hollywood came director Howard Hawks and his willowy attractive wife, called Slim; producer Leland Hayward and his actress wife Margaret Sullavan, who liked to be called Maggie; the handsome actor Robert knew that he didn't expect me to get them together, and he seemed in no hurry, so I went into a brief dissertation on the Labrador dogs he'd given the Valley, said that I was sure he'd hear praise of them to make mine dull. He thanked me and went on his way. Late that afternoon I saw him in the lobby; he took the trouble to say how right I was about the dogs, and the praise he got on the great Idaho hunting. I said I had a hunch he might be going afield. He grinned, said, "We might, at that."

We hadn't gone out that day, and sure enough Papa told me that he and Taylor were to take the big boss and Kathleen on the canoe run down Silver Creek, separately in relay, that Mr. Harriman had sent for guns. I said, "You're quite the promoter, Papa." No, he said, he had just told the truth of how it was — great stuff, and it was good duck weather right then, a little rainy, and they'd hold good on the creek. They did, on a wet cold day, the only hunt they made, a good one.

Now the punch line, a Papa tale, but it rang true.

He admitted, when he was on the throne, that he had overreached himself and his gun, made some good shots, and missed a few. Then, in his well-meaning blunt way, Mr. Harriman told him that he was lightly disappointed in him — didn't quite come up to his reputation as an unbeatable shot.

I laughed outright when he told me about it — so familiar, I said — and asked his retort.

"I kept my mouth shut, for once, but I wanted to say, 'Well, Averell, just how damn long did you play the game to rate as a seven-goal man at polo?' "

"Well, why didn't you, Papa?"

"Because what I know about polo you can stuff in a .410 shotgun shell and have room left for what I know about a balloon."

Anyway, Mr. Harriman apparently accomplished in his behind-the-scenes way what management had been urging on Papa for some time — a move over to Glamour

House, which both he and Marty missed so much. The Inn was all right at first, but when the weather concentrated the horde of tame ducks on the big lagoon so close to their quarters, their morning clamoring was not so good when Papa worked early at his correspondence.

Late that fall there was a gathering of

the notables at the Trail Creek Cabin. At the time it appeared that Howard Hawks was a cinch to direct the filming of *For Whom the Bell Tolls* for Paramount, and the principal roles were decided upon, though there was *no* insistence by Papa on Coop and Ingrid Bergman as Robert Jordan and Maria. Yes, his preference was an influence,

In Silver Creek's sloughs a greenwing teal and a fat mallard are taken by Papa's Browning.

Papa and Coop watching their dogs retrieve mallards.

but he did not tamper "in the face of such a hell of a deal I got on it." So that was the subject, then it gradually evolved into a favorite topic — boxing — due to a recent event involving Papa and us locals (too lengthy for space here). We were all feeling the glow and soon a few were taking mild swings at the Hemingway midriff — muscles that he could tighten up like a rock; nor was he hesitant, when in the right mood, to challenge your hitting power. He laughingly challenged the willful good sport Howard Hawks, who delivered a haymaker.

News of the disaster at Pearl Harbor reached us. A couple of days later Papa and Marty pulled away in the Lincoln. He decided he would rig the *Pilar* to hunt U-Boats in the Caribbean and Gulf Stream.

In June of 1942 I enlisted in the Air Force, was bounced around to half a dozen bases, and Tillie finally joined me in San Antonio. We gasped when we picked up the June 26, 1944 issue of *Life* magazine, to see the full-page Robert Capa picture of Papa Hemingway in a London hospital bed, wearing a tremendous beard, his head swathed in a turbanlike bandage fastened by safety pins. The caption said he was the correspondent Hemingway, and had managed to provide copy for the rest of the correspondents by becoming an indirect casualty of the second front. Read on: On his way to his quarters from a sober party a few nights before the invasion, his car crashed into an unlighted water tank in the middle of a blacked-out London street. Hemingway, the driver and a passenger and the water tank spilled all over the road; the brawny novelist landed in the hospital where surgeons put fifty-two stitches in his pate!

"Good God!" Tillie said to me. "Enough to sew back the whole top of his head . . . poor old Papa, and it says that from the mess he's got water on the knee, and they say he's forty-six . . . he won't be forty-five until next month."

The caption said that he had already landed with invasion forces on the Normandy beachheads and was flying missions with the R.A.F. and that Marty was also covering the war as a correspondent.

That fifty-two stitches business bothered us no end, but I had to smile when I remembered him saying, "I won't sit aside and watch." I had joked him about being the old fire horse answering the bell when last

with him; he had tapped his knee, said with a laugh, "You saw me run once with it. Maybe I can again if I'm out front and scared."

We don't remember just when it was that we stood in line for tickets to see *For Whom the Bell Tolls*, but we do remember whispering to each other that they opened the film exactly as Papa had predicted: "They'll have to do it Hollywood style, you'll see, the scriptwriters will blow the train right off, instead of it opening quietly in the forest as I wrote it . . . and ended it."

After the war was over we heard that Papa Hemingway was in Cuba, his marriage broken up. That pained us, remembering the great times with Marty, whom we still speak of as a "hell of a gal," the kind you never forget. However, we felt that we understood how it was, and perhaps even how it might have been, from our knowledge of both of them, from the beginning: too much alike. Though it was only a joking remark at the time, we thought it ironical when we heard of the breakup: "I look like I'm pointing to the dark future."

Bumby Hemingway, out of the service after a harrowing time as a prisoner of war, came out in the fall of 1945 to pick up his old car left in Sun Valley, and to check on the curriculum at the University of Montana — a long day's drive — at Missoula. Bumby stayed with us, we talked ourselves hoarse, and so got the report pretty much firsthand on so many things, including an indirect introduction to former correspondent Mary Welsh, whom Papa had met in London when she was on the staff of *Time* magazine. Shortly after Bumby left for Cuba in early December we got word of the Hemingway-Gellhorn divorce. A Christmas greeting from Papa said that there would be a wedding before long — but no date had been set.

In early March of 1946 Bumby came down from school in Missoula, stayed with us, and we rustled about and got him fitted out for some skiing. During his stay with us,

Mary Welsh became Mrs. Ernest Hemingway. There were telegrams exchanged, and some laughs at a news picture of the couple, of which Bumby said that he'd never seen his father so nicely gussied up as he was in his dark, pin-striped double-breasted wedding suit. We hadn't either, and no one enjoyed our comments about it more than Papa.

By late July I was receiving boxes of gear shipped from Key West and searching for suitable living quarters in town at Papa's instructions. In his letters and a phone call, he stressed economy, said he'd had an expensive time of it getting organizoots again at the Finca (his home in Cuba), and felt there was no better place to start off the new era with his family all together than in Idaho, hunting and living the simple life. He said "Miss Mary" was a fair cook, so I was to find something with a good kitchen in it, and as much privacy as possible; use my own judgment, get it for three months starting on September 1 — "We're going to make it for the dove shooting, at last!"

Just across Trail Creek, outside of town, was the best setup I knew of: MacDonald's log cabins in a long row set back from the highway. Mac was redoing his modest comfortable owner's quarters for long-term rental purposes, so I was lucky in timing, got it tied up in mid-August when Bumby Hemingway and the younger boys arrived to "make out" with Taylor in his little bailiwick — with sleeping bags — and get with the fishing.

Dusk one evening I was at home alone, resting on the porch from mowing the grass. In greeting me as if it hadn't been years, the tone of Papa's voice over the phone told me there was something seriously wrong.

"Pappy, we're delayed over here in Casper, and in trouble . . . Mary's in the hospital following emergency surgery . . . almost lost her and she's not out of the woods yet, but we think that she'll make it. . . ."

He did not tell me what it was, and I didn't ask. He said he couldn't know how long the delay would be, and to speak to the boys about it in a way that wouldn't spoil their fun if I could.

By September 11 Mary was able to travel, and on the twelfth I got a telegram from Cody, Wyoming, on the favored old route west:

PLANNING TO ARRIVE FRIDAY EVENING LOVE TO ALL PAPA.

4.

Mary Hemingway's Debut

How often we've laughed with Mary in recalling her introduction to the upper Wood River community, part of it old as the hills and known everywhere as Sun Valley, Idaho. The faithful old Lincoln got them here a bit after five o'clock, they checked in at the cabins, okayed them, then by what Papa called our private connection road he followed me and drove right up to our front porch. Like she was a doll, he picked Mary up in his arms and took her into our kitchen where a well-cushioned, old-fashioned rocking chair awaited her — on the far side of the room opposite the old cookstove that I had fired up good to heat the oven for a heaping platter of mourning doves for the

The Hemingway fall pantry.

welcoming meal. Mary's obvious embarrassment at meeting strangers this way was short-lived. Papa as good as knew my parents, who happened to be staying with us, addressed them as Mom and Bill, and he felt as much at home as the boys. An immediate remark was an apology for arriving on Friday the thirteenth! But he looked at the platter of birds, the heaping dishpan of the little fruit that the boys and I had picked on "damson plum lane" while dove hunting, and he said, "But, by the looks of things it might be good luck now, Mom's going to make jams and jellies . . . the best there is with good wild red meat."

I fixed him with a whimsical look. His eyes twinkled.

"Come on, let old Papa in on it."

"Double the thirteenth," I said. "On the twenty-sixth I've got a date with a Pahsimeroi antelope."

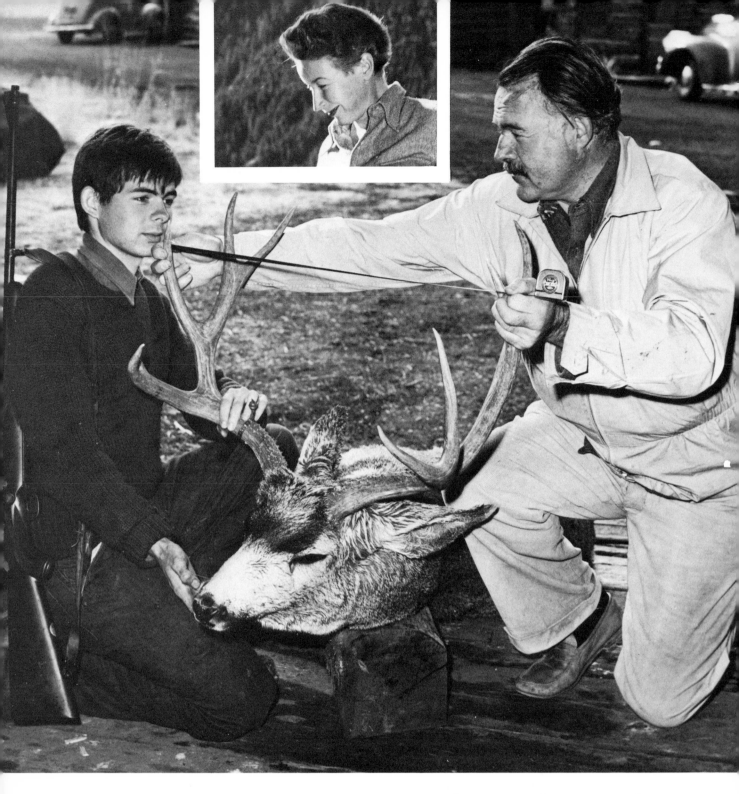

October, 1946. Patrick Hemingway's first big game, taken with his father's old Springfield. Insert: "Miss Mary"—the Hemingway bride of the previous March.

On the twenty-sixth I got my antelope buck — a fat young meat animal — in two shots. I slid off my horse and missed him clean at a long hundred yards, on a ridge that he calmly walked off of before I could bolt another cartridge into the chamber. I ran but went prone because of the distance to make my steady-rest shot, panting like a lizard. My bullet literally cut his throat at three hundred and twenty-six carefully paced steps. With me was a young Sun Valley staffer just back from the war named Jimmy Saviers. Jimmy was my confirmation that night when we got home and I told Papa Hemingway of my crazy shooting. I got his typical response.

"Well, I put the good sign on, didn't I? And that was great shooting, kid, for true . . . but the colonel and me got you beat yet . . . we both made ours with borrowed rifles!"

"Rub it in, Papa, you so-and-so," I said as we hung up the split-down-the-back buck in a big rickety airy old barn in back of Mac's cabins, which, he said, we were welcome to use for hanging game for aging, and ducks and upland birds heads up for the curing that tenderizes and enhances the flavor. The nights were frosty sharp by then, the old barn held the temperature well during the warm days — a perfect setup but thirty feet from the kitchen door. In the first days of deer season I slipped out one morning and got a small spike buck while Taylor took Patrick Hemingway up into an old area of his and the boy got a handsome well-antlered buck in perfect meat condition. He used his father's old Springfield that he practically slept with for days beforehand; and, indeed, Papa was proud that on his first try at big game, Patrick was the meat-getter; and that his good friend with the know-how showed him just where to place his bullet for a one-shot kill.

Economy was stressed, and we were off to a good start at living off the country. Austerity was a necessity with us, too, for we were pouring every cent we had into the building of a home for my parents. Papa went up with me one day to look it over — perched on the hillside of an undeveloped part of town that was yet only a village. Deeply respectful of our strong filial ties, he said, "Doing what you are for your folks is not covered by a couple of well-worn ones like loyalty and duty. You're going about it as a privilege, and that is something that is to be envied . . . it's so rare in families."

"That's a great compliment, Papa," I said. "But then, too, we're the sort that like a table of our own to put our feet under, remember?"

"Yeah, I know, but what I said still holds good in my book . . . you'll always feel good about it, I can tell you that."

During the dove season, and later in the month, a situation developed that permanently altered relations already tainted. The railroad's colorful President Jeffers had retired early in the year and now there was one of an entirely different sort at the throttle. A small, officious man, he was a Jekyll and Hyde type who could make things quite rough when in the latter garb. He fancied himself a hunter, which he was not, nor was he physically up to it most of the times that we saw him. With none of his guides back yet, Taylor took the new president and his companion down and introduced them to the dove country, all that he was asked to do. Then in a couple of days the game warden called on him with bona fide reports from ranchers in Silver Creek basin that the railroad's president, of all people, was seen riding the fenders of his car, shooting doves on the go — a flagrant disregard for the law, which could throw the book at him for such. The warden was a friend of Taylor and to Sun Valley, the relations record a flawless one, much of it to the colonel's credit. It was up to him to handle it quietly, and he did, but firmly — there would be no more of that.

The next upset of the fall was not long in coming. Down in Hollywood, producer Mark Hellinger took the great Hemingway short story — "The Killers" — and with vivid imagination in scripting, rounded it out as a first-rate full-length movie — the one that put Burt Lancaster in the big time. Mark himself brought a print of it up to

Ketchum for a little "premiere" for the author. At the time our movie "Opera House" was in a state of overhaul, one projector only operable, the rear-screen speakers removed for replacement. Mark had to return the print quickly so I got our electrician and we rigged up a makeshift system. The sound was not so bad, but the effect was awful — compounded by projection interruptions for reel change — for the man who had a notorious

Mary and Papa holding some of Idaho's plentiful pheasants.

dislike for Hollywood versions of his work. This one he lauded, asked for a rerun of one particular reel. In fact, he joked that he liked the picture so much he was tempted to redo "The Killers" in full-length form himself. He and Mark had a long-term deal on the fire for other Hemingway stories.

Their deal was wrapped up after the showing, then Mark was around for several days, staying at a new combination motel-restaurant gambling-casino place at the outskirts of town called the Thunderbird. It's rather ironical that a notable member of the prewar shooting tribe had a sizable interest in the club where Mark went on his gay and expensive spree. Mark Hellinger was fleeced, and set himself up for it, but good. Papa Hemingway tried his best to avert it — I know, for I was there when he would not touch a drop with Mark. All men run their course in such, and finally Mark returned to California. In ten days we got the news of his sudden death from a heart attack.

For a day or so, Papa said little about it. Then he let go a flood coming up from the creek one night in a cold rain. He flatly said that he had feared something like this, but could not understand why Mark had to go off the deep end. But in his "glory hole" (his pocket, a desk drawer, or maybe a cardboard box, for safekeeping) was Mark's check to him — a sizable one of five figures that anyone else would have deposited before the ink was dry. But maybe he had his reason in that case. Whatever, he returned the check to Mark's widow. In return for his decency and fair play, he never received an acknowledgment.

What we heard about the whole thing, in sum, was this: That had the deal with Hellinger been carried out as planned, over the long pull it meant "so much dough that I'm almost afraid to think about it."

Like us, he was worried about another angle over the long pull. "It's a bad thing, taking a guy like that. But damn it, after a war there are always changes, elements that move in and give places like this a black eye. Let's hope it doesn't spread like a disease and spoil it."

The departure for Cuba was the day after Christmas, with a stopover in Salt Lake City to visit old friend Charlie Sweeney who'd been up for a visit in the fall. Had there not been considerable gear stored in the lockable attic in our shell of a house, it would have been an easy matter to think we might not see Mary and Papa the coming fall. Several times he'd said he'd have to get into production on something pretty quick; he was "runnin' outa credit a little too fast." But Mary was in fine shape then, had been for a long time, and when we saw them off that morning they both said, "It will be great if we can make it by September 1."

Papa Hemingway hooked on Sun Valley territory.

5.

The Good Postwar Fall

During the '47 winter, Taylor Williams bubbled with enthusiasm for his spring trip to fish the Florida Keys. The correspondence flowed between him and Cuba, for Papa Hemingway had made quite a to-do about him coming over for a good go with him in the Gulf Stream — on the *Pilar*. Taylor had always made most of his fly rods and now he was knee-deep in heavy saltwater rods — beautifully done, too. In late winter I photographed them, made letter-size prints, then typed a long letter for him, advising his host that on April 1 he'd be on his way, with his shotgun, too, for the fantastic Cuban dove shooting. Papa's replies to him made you ask yourself which was the bigger kid of the two, and wish that you could be included in on the deal.

Fate, however, dealt the colonel another blow. He was at our door one morning before we were dressed, so stunned that he couldn't speak, handing us the telegram advising of the sudden death of his daughter Betty in Arizona. I don't recall ever seeing a more shaken man. His family was wiped out but for a single grandchild and his one surviving son, Bob, a seafaring man living in Portland, Oregon; a loyal son, indeed, but remote from his father because of his work. Self-reliant from the core as a rule, Taylor was no good now: I got his emergency rail passes for him, almost packed his bag, to get him on his way. At the bus he asked if I would write Papa and tell him he might be a bit delayed — if he could make it at all.

I cabled a brief message, followed it up with a special-delivery letter. I got a phone call from Papa immediately. His word: Do everything humanly possible, calling upon him if need be, to see the colonel on his way south. He said, "He needs it, Pappy, he's had enough grief. Find out what you can and let me know." I promised that, but the loss hit Taylor in more ways than one, and upon his return he was on the fence about going. We talked about it at length, and in the interim I got off a brief cable. A second phone call came, this one to the colonel, and on April 1 he was on his way. With little demand for fishing guides before late June, he returned in time, with the old spring in his step. Had some orders for me, too, which I discharged at once.

It was September 20 when Papa and the boys arrived in a new Buick Roadmaster convertible. Mary was to arrive in a few days by air — for there was some difficulty, or suspicion, on the part of the Cuban government about excessive arms at the Finca. Papa snorted about it, and a ruse of some sort was figured in getting the favored guns out of the country. Naturally, there was the beat-up old pump gun and the faithful Browning double among the load, but he had a sad story to tell me. He had forgotten to bring the Duke of Alba shotgun the previous fall, for he had not changed his mind about passing it on to me. On a dove shoot he'd loaned it to a guest, and the man's carrier boy stumbled with it, plugging both muzzles with mud. On the next drive of birds the friend cut loose with it — no barrels left! Papa was sick about it, would have sent it to the Spanish makers for new barrels, but he wasn't exactly a hero in Spain, following the civil war and the "book." But the kick was, he brought along the little 6.5 Mannlicher we'd won on the raffle in '41.

"She's done me all the good she can, which was little, so you don't owe me a half-bottle . . . we don't know what it accounted for when the cook had it, but it has a shark to its credit now — a big fish-eating shark."

(Though the little rifle has accounted for very little for me, it has an honored place in my rack today.)

For two good reasons of his own, Papa stayed with Mary up at Glamour House until October 15, then returned to the MacDonald cabins that I had reserved for them — austerity again stressed. But the old ebullient Papa was with us again, in sharp contrast to the fall before, and how good it was to see. Because of his high blood pressure and weight problem, Papa heeded Dr. Moritz' advice: not to even think about going into the higher country for big game. I had neither the time nor the money to go for elk, so I hunted mornings for a deer while Taylor guided Mary for a first try at big game with a rifle.

Papa and I got our heads together with Bud Purdy, who earlier had suggested an outlying summer ranch of his not far from the Craters of the Moon country — an open, high-rolling wintering area for deer.

At four o'clock in the morning of Friday, October 17, Mary got breakfast while Papa whipped up lunch sandwiches for us, in his pajamas and robe. We had fifty miles to drive up into the foothills of country we could not hunt by horse because of its openness. Well before sunrise we climbed steadily on shank's mare, Mary's wind much improved since her arrival at the approximate six-thousand-foot level. Miles later we topped out on a high bare knob of a miniature mountain with no choice but to sit there for a bite of lunch and some needed rest, and to glass a vast sweep of country with my binoculars.

Far down in a wide, exposed canyon — about two miles — something moved in a small stand of aspens. It turned out to be a fat doe, barren of that year's fawn by her color. She moved out from the midday siesta, looked about, then straight into my glasses. "Don't move a muscle, Mary, we'll have to sweat her out, hope that she'll start to browse on that gentle slope above the creek." She did, and there was a glint of movement in the aspen gold — sun glint on a head of polished antlers! The rut was well past and this fellow should be in fine shape — if he'd only move out for a good look at him. We had it made — if we could get off that knob an inch at a time, as cats do in stalking a bird, and over to a dry, twisting gully of countless spring runoffs draining the whole face of our big hill down into that little creek. We accomplished it somehow — time and patience — and started down on as tough a stalk as a hunter could find. In an hour or so we made it, peeked over a drop-off, screened by brush, to appraise a fine buck at some two hundred yards below us — a forty-five-degree down-angle shot that is toughest of all with a rifled weapon. The buck stood broadside, sniffing the air suspiciously, his attention down the canyon, the does in the aspens. I wanted one of them for meat.

Then both our spirits sank to zero when down the canyon a rifle shot rang out — not too far off, and it sounded to me like the familiar old "thutty-thutty" caliber. A critical moment — the buck jumped a few yards, held it, his radar in full operation; not a second to lose. Mary lined up on him, as best I could tell her, and, yes, she said, "Back me up." I did, but needn't have: her shot stopped him cold, then he moved with the shock and I put him down with the advantage of my 'scope over her aperture sights. We scrambled, fell down the steepness, then a doe broke out for a clean shot and I got her.

Who the hell wanted it that way? Sorry, Mary, but your bullet was first. Never mind, at four in the afternoon her handsomely antlered buck and the fat doe were field-dressed when a man and his wife came footing it up the creek and the woman said that she had taken a shot at an owl in a tree. She carried a battered .30-30 Winchester carbine; I could have beaten her with it!

The '47 fall produced an absolute first: Old Silver Creek finally won a round on its terms. Old Stutter Man's place was forlorn and deserted, and we felt a twinge of conscience when we heard that in the war years someone had missed seeing him around, then discovered him dead in his bed. Two old bachelor brothers took over the place, rather odd characters, but friendly enough; they had no objection at all to our shooting the ridge for ducks. We saw to it that they had ducks for their table. Then one miserable cold day, Papa and Bumby floated the usual run in a keeled mate to our little *Stutter Bug* canoe that was lost in some way as a Navy casualty of war. At pullout they were short a few birds and decided to explore the winding stretch of the creek below Stutter bridge, about a long half-mile of it to the lower highway bridge where the creek flows out of the basin. None of us knew it, of course, except from the highway and the down view from the ridge. To fly fisherman Bumby it looked good for another year; there were ducks, too. Also, it proved deceptive in current and speed. They got within a hundred yards of the highway where, on a sharp bend, the canoe was incapable of bending, and over she went, dumping the works in some ten feet of water. Papa was in hip boots, Bumby in chest-high waders, but there was no problem due to the narrowness of the stream, on whose amalgam bottom lay the Browning over-under and the old Winchester pump — the veteran with the proverbial nine lives of a cat.

I knew nothing of the mishap until the following night around seven. Just putting on my coat to go and eat, then return to finish a small job, I heard a rap on a big end window of the living room. A glance at Papa's face peering in from the dark plainly said: We're in a bit of trouble. I let him in and he told me all about it, cursing himself and things in general — with a laugh in it, too. He said that when he felt his butt hit that water for a complete immersion, he swore that it was the hand of old Stutter's spook he saw pulling the canoe out from under them. It struck my funny bone so that I sat down on a sawhorse and let the laughter rip so hard that I thought my company might stalk out on me.

"Yeah, and to think of the times we've

run 'er, then pull a stunt like we did. . . ."

"That spring-fed water gets awful cold after some miles on the surface, doesn't it, Papa?"

"Jesus! Make an Eskimo drop his teeth." He laughed and pulled a flask from his pocket, looked around at the mess I had to get ready for our winter occupancy — or bust, figuratively speaking.

New Year's Eve, 1947. Clockwise from lower left: *Papa, director Henry Hathaway, Gary Cooper, and Ingrid Bergman.*

Christmas night in Sun Valley, 1947.

"Think you'll make it before you open up at the Valley, or maybe by Christmas, kid?"

"I'd better, Papa. I ran the loafers I've been paying off the job today. Once they get inside where it's warm, you know. . . ."

"Sure, they let you have it below the belt. . . . Then you'll get it done, I know you will, here's to it."

Well as he shot his old standbys, and understood their functioning, Papa was simply out of the running on things mechanical. Now he apologized for coming to me for help in disassembling his guns completely for the cleanup, and since I'd partaken in so little of the duck shooting but had shared the loot, I said, wasn't that too bad? Tillie was already at his place. Dinner was in hatch. So, to keep it safe and not blow the place with fumes of high-test gasoline for washing gun parts, we took to the airy barn with cracks in its walls you could pitch a cat through, and poured a little hi-test into ourselves as we worked — for what is colder on bare hands than highly evaporative fuel in near-zero weather? By midnight or thereabouts the guns worked smoothly again, and the hunters were back in business. I had a loyal helper every minute, who said, "Hell with that," when I suggested he go to bed. It was a split duck season and there was little left of the first half.

Not long afterwards we got a pleasant surprise: Papa announced that their quarters were available into the winter and they would stay over until perhaps all of January. Mary expressed an urge to try her legs on skis, and had already done a little shopping in that direction. So what in hell are you going to take up, Papa?

90

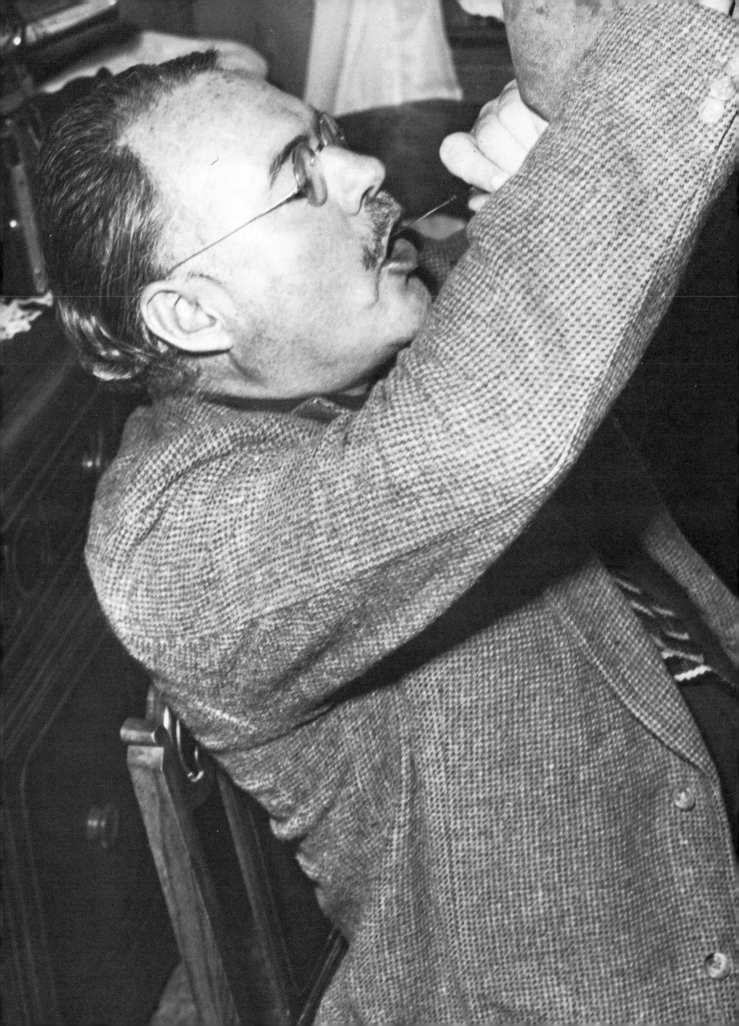

Coop proves he can inhale it with a cigarette in his
mouth.

Left: Inhaling the red.

"Snow shoveling." He chuckled, patting his impressive paunch. "I might hire out to the city, keep the walks open to the joints in the block . . . the Rio Club, I'll do for free." (The Rio was the Stockmen's Saloon of the old days — run by Basques still, and a favorite always.)

For the holidays, and well into January, there were gentleman guests up from Cuba: scholarly young Roberto Herrara, and seagoing merchant ship captain Juan "Sinsky" Duñabeitia. Roberto's English was passable anywhere, Sinsky's a language of its own — but who ever heard of Spanish-English language barriers in a house of Hemingway's?

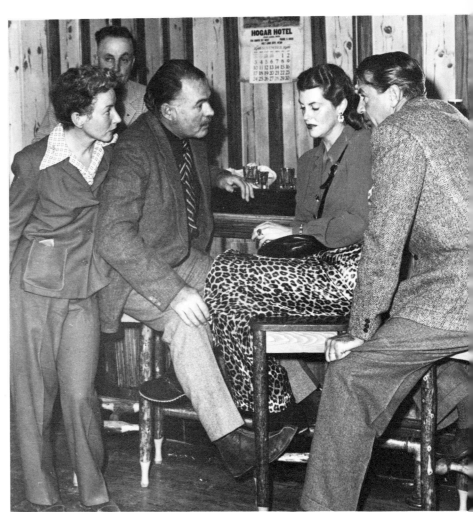

The Hemingways and Coopers having a nightcap.

New Year's Eve crowd of 1947.

The usual New Year crowd poured in; Hollywood was never so well represented. Old Sun Valley was really jumping that gay winter. The year 1947 went out in a wild whoopee with an elite event at Trail Creek Cabin. That party Papa Hemingway readily consented they attend, admitting more curiosity than anything else. Without doubt, most of his interest was focused on Ingrid Bergman. His table was a corner one in the big room, and if either of them left it for hours on end I don't remember it. Coop was a frequent stopper, joining the intent conversation, the laughs, sipping at the inexhaustible champagne. Before the meal was over, Papa's jacket came off; he wore a soft wool shirt of neat pattern weave, but left his tie snugged up where it belonged — "Goddamnit . . . hot in this noisy place!" — and remained in his shirt sleeves until the party faded out in the wee hours. Much has been reported of the author joking of Robert Jordan making love in the sleeping bag, with his shirt on, and that is when and where it was done. So far as I know that is the only time the three were together — the author and co-stars of the movie version of F.W.T.B.T.

But that was about the sum of the social side of the simple life; Papa made no bones about avoiding involvement: "too rich for my blood, right now." His friends stayed until well into January. One snowy day early in the month he came stomping into the shop and one look at him prompted my question. He said, yes, in many ways he was enjoying his first winter visit, but time did seem to hang a bit heavy occasionally. Quite sure that I read him true, I tucked it away for the time being. Coop skied quite a lot in those days, as much to hold up his part of "being in the swim" as anything; he could take it or leave it — by a varmint rifle shot any day! After so much of it the old hip injury would begin to bother him. Then he'd be among the missing in the ski lift or chow line at the Roundhouse on the big mountain. Often in past winters in the stormy times I took an occasional day to prowl about the lower country with him in quest of a few jackrabbits or a bobcat in the lava beds. I was encouraged by management to do so if my program permitted. So, sure enough, it wasn't long until Coop came to the shop one cold morning to tell me he got a fine "bobkitty" the day before; it was a good pelt that he'd have made into a little bedside rug for little daughter Maria — to match one she already had from an Idaho kitty. He wondered if someone could take a picture of him with it. Someone did, then and there, and he asked me when I might sneak a day or two with him. I read him true, also. Sure, I could, any time, and had he seen or called Papa Hemingway, who might like to do a little prowling too? Yeah, he'd seen him, but maybe he was working too hard. By the same token, Papa wouldn't interfere with Coop's skiing, and didn't know that he'd about had his fill of it for that year. I said to Coop, "Try him, and see."

Tillie just picked up her phone and called Papa, said Coop wanted to talk to him. I thought to myself: Funny, these two, their first time together in the community, in circumstances different than in their accustomed falls, when everything is automatically a cut-and-dried proposition.

So, for the balance of the Coopers' stay there were several good prowls; the lower country seldom had more than a hint of snow. On his off days from his relief checker's job on the ski lifts, Taylor joined us. On his insistence we used Papa's Buick. Being a convertible, it was easy to shoot from with all the windows down. Against the law? Well, out in the open, miles from nowhere, and "on the prod fer a pesky er vicious varmint" in Coop language? So, like in the movies, Papa rode shotgun, I did most of the driving, and I'm sure I needn't say that ours was largely a foursome of kids at the cowboys-and-Indians stuff. Which is exactly how it was on one of the prowls — as much by accident as plan.

Both Papa and Coop had often

expressed their curiosity about the historic Oregon Trail where, beyond upper Hagerman Valley, it skirts the Snake River bluffs, then cuts across a vast desert plateau to storied Three Island Crossing, many miles farther downstream. Nothing much to see, it nonetheless awakens something in the imagination of romantics. For some botanical reason the sagebrush along the ridges of the numerous and deeply eroded ruts of empire grew tall as a man on a horse, and by sight alone you could follow the trail for miles. It was Taylor who said that jackrabbits liked those ruts — shelter from the incessant wind — and coyotes were always around. Cruise parallel to it, and there could be some action. For miles we saw nothing, then doubled back and topped a low rise close to where we'd started. There was Mr. Coyote trotting toward us at an angle, heading for the tall sage rows. He changed his angle and would have made it, but the big Buick was a powerhouse and cut him off. Like a furry streak he took off across the open country toward a slope of normal sage a good mile away. Papa yelled, "Take after the bastard, step on it!"

I hesitated, but heard the action of his gun slam a shell home, a rifle bolt locking behind us, seconding his motion. I tromped on it with a heavy foot and the smooth land ahead was ten times as rough as it looked. I hoped that the springs and tires would hold. By a miracle they did, but I was hard put in catching that coyote and dared not get too close — he'd turn on a dime and the chase would be over. The old pump gun barked a couple of times to keep the pursued in the notion and the protection of the sage was coming up too fast. I saw an open spot ahead, slammed on the brakes in a skidding stop and a cloud of dust and Coop lowered the boom on him in a dead straightaway shot.

"Pretty fancy shootin', that, Mr. Cooper!"

"Did a little yerself, podner . . . saw him take on about seven knots per when you nicked him with a few . . . and pretty fair herdin' this hoss, did we say Tallyho, there goes?"

"I guess, and I'm almost afraid to open the hoss's door," I said. "It might fall off the hinges."

"Aw, we didn't hurt 'er none." Papa grinned. "It was worth tearin' up a Deusenberg for, huh, Coop?"

6.

The Fall of '48

When Taylor Williams returned from his spring trek to the Keys and Cuba there was a shadow of a doubt that Papa Hemingway would come West that fall. It was not a spectacular era in the waterfowl history of our continent. Spring hatches were down and it was known that we'd have another split shooting season that would not be attractive time-wise. But in contrast to the overall situation, the local one was good for ducks. So when the dates were published we mailed them to Cuba immediately and were a bit surprised by the immediate response: Coming anyway — line up the MacDonald cabin setup again. The

Coop with a "pesky varmint."

waterfowl dates: October 29 to November 14 — December 23 to January 8. Tucked between was the upland bird season of exactly three weeks ending November 21. So what does an all-outer do in shotgun country in a full "dry" month of the fall?

The arrival was a late one — mid-October — and we had the pantry well stocked for an appetizer and some main fare. By then it was something of a joke about always missing the dove season, but it was now a well-established institution — you weren't in the swim if you didn't "shoot them little things" which made little things out of quite a few who talked awful good gunning, and knocked you down to get to the table ahead of you. But it was the colonel who took the kidding of his life for how he bagged the big meat. The small crew, who in summer "manicured" ski trails on the big mountain, reported to him that a big lone mule deer buck holed up during the day in a small stand of pines in the "Bowl Area." Well, he'd be damned if that wasn't a square deal, so he — of all people, who scorned all but the old-school ways — hopped on the ski lift with the crew and had the big buck down squarely in the middle of Easter Bowl, on a 50 percent grade, by eight o'clock in the morning. Big as a small elk and in perfect condition, it took four of us to pole-pack him down to where we could drive a jeep. That was a short week before the Hemingway arrival.

"I wonder if it will do me any good to ask if there's any of the liver left?"

The inevitable snort: "Who knows better than you that deer liver spoils in twenty-four hours unless you eat it."

Mr. Williams drooled for a solid year for that treat — he and a lot of others — and leave his method to him: it took me several days to collect a little one-spiker that I could pack in on my back alone. There was liver left, but it had to be joked about.

The younger boys missed that fall, and Bumby got in but a few days of pheasant shooting — waiting his call for another tour of duty with the Army. The first half of the duck season was excellent, and we had Silver Creek practically to ourselves, Mary and Papa making good use of the canoe trip. The Frees farm area was also pretty much ours but generally the lower country was under heavy hunting pressure; weekends were something to avoid, and though the bird population was as good as ever, the wily pheasant was just a mite wiser. Nonetheless, we ate as good as ever. Then the dry December rolled around and there was an on-the-fence interim about staying on for Christmas, our attempts at persuasion not at all subtle. We lost, and we knew that ahead was a period of absenteeism; we had known for a long time that it was inevitable.

We got it all at once, sitting around the table one evening — a very gay one, reminiscing more than usual. After he announced that he hoped they'd not have to miss more than two falls, Papa asked about our attic room. It was all his, we told him, and asked how his supply of pencils was.

"Oh, if times get rougher I'll send up for a hatful, or if I dig around I might still have some from that hatful you guys loaded me with."

(We had — in '39, when he settled down to work — wished him good luck when several of us showed up at Glamour House, each with a pocketful of "company issue" pencils. He dumped them all in the old Afrikaner Stetson, picked up a cased fly rod, said that if we'd have it painted white he'd work the streets on Saturday nights and get off relief.)

There was little doubt of his intent; he said he had the outline of a big work in his head and it might take him two years to do it, so a small truckload of gear was stored with us: rifles, fishing rods never used but once, sleeping bags, a tent, boxes of odds and ends, and two small trunks of clothing — plus a very nice roomy bookcase that Sun Valley's carpenter shop made for him when they were in Glamour House the short time the previous fall. He left about a hundred books with it, and I joked with him that if he left the stuff more than a couple of years I'd charge him rent.

"Let's see, now, what is your favorite brand?" He laughed. "But we'll do our best, kid, and maybe when the colonel is down in the spring we'll know more then."

The departure was on December 15.

During the winter Mary wrote that they would soon head for Europe, and she gave us the Paris address of the Guaranty Trust Company for mail forwarding. From an earlier hint only, we bet on northern Italy, which it proved to be: old haunts country, Cortina D'Ampezzo the hub, mostly. Later we got it by public news that Papa had a serious infection from a bit of shotgun wadding blown into his eye by wind while hunting on the marshes near Venice. Their intent of a few weeks' trip stretched to nine

Comb-harpist Hemingway.

months, in which *Across the River and Into the Trees* was largely written. Neglect on our part is reason for correspondence being almost nil.

The new novel was serialized in *Cosmopolitan* magazine, but we were damned if we'd read Papa in installments this time. We read John O'Hara's review in the *New York Times* issue of September 10. But when we got our hardcover copy inscribed by the author later in the fall, his inscription didn't hold a warm personal candle to those in the six volumes of the special "Sunrise Edition" by Scribner's back in '39. Oh, it was personal enough, but that "touch" wasn't there. Two falls in absentia. How many more? I, for one, with good reason, felt there would be plenty. I was certain of it when in the summer of '51 he sent us "The Shot" story and wished he could come out to spend the dough with us that fall.

Remember his remark that I reported at the time of Mark Hellinger's tragedy: ". . . let's hope it doesn't spread like a disease and spoil it." Another one, much farther back: he "spooks easy." Well, Papa Hemingway was, basically, just about as spooky as they come — perhaps because of the uncanny accuracy of the crystal ball between his ears. Our little community did split its pants seams in a fizzling-out postwar bust; certain of the newer-element boys got a bit greedy running their games of chance; there were justifiable complaints that got to out-of-state competitive ears, and plenty of in-state ears, too, that had been awaiting the chance to pounce. So the law cracked down on the always illegal gambling, and out went a way of life that fit the country, as we knew it in the older days. It was this change that caused Papa Hemingway to flatly say that he doubted he'd ever return to Idaho. He was not an addict of gambling; it was simply a carry-over of the Old West to him, an expression of individual freedom, and if hurt, it was your own damn fault.

When Taylor Williams returned from Cuba in June of '52, we saw him hop off the bus almost before it stopped rolling, and come down the path to our shop in a half dogtrot. Oh, oh, is it glad tidings this time? From his jacket pocket he pulled our copy of *The Old Man and the Sea*. We had read it in *Life*, in spite of our avowal, and we were almost afraid to open it to see what the

Taylor Williams, Mary, and Ernest on location in Cuba for The Old Man and the Sea.

"write something in it" was.

*For Pappy and Tilly
with much love*
     PAPA
*We miss you awfully bad;
  the worst Time is the fall of the year.
  Please kiss Miss Tilly for me*
                    PAPA:
ERNEST HEMINGWAY — Finca Vigia
                    — 1952

In late spring of '53, while Taylor was in Cuba, I got a letter from him and Papa, telling me to ship things to the stateside outfitter, Abercrombie & Fitch in New York, for the second African safari that Papa and Mary planned after a summer trip to Spain. Taylor requested that I ship his Model 70 Winchester .270-caliber for Mary — stock to be fitted to her by Griffin & Howe — and his heavy Colt target revolver. From Papa's glory hole in our attic went the old Springfield .30-06, a couple of plinking rifles, and heavy clothing. In Papa's letter was a warming long paragraph wishing I could go along: "Your good eyes, and my good nose, and your long lenses and that movie box that you shoot like a gun . . . hell, we might go into business." I laughed because of his crack about his nose, which was, indeed, a good one, and not because I thought I was being salved. I had fun putting little notes in pockets of the old latigo leather vest and the folded flat-as-a-pancake old Stetson hat.

The visit to Spain that summer was the first since 1939, and a thank-you note from Nairobi in late August said that his welcome was surprising, and pleasing. The next news, of course, was of the African plane crashes in January of '54. Like Hemingway history

says, the obituaries were all ready for release (some of them were out) when the truth of it finally came. It scared hell out of us, and an aviation expert was on hand who feared it more. Pete and Dorothy Hill had come over from Idaho Falls to see us, and Cessna airplanes were part of his business. When he heard that it was a 180 type with spring-steel legs on its fixed landing gear, well, he thought that in brushy terrain that craft would be flipped over with a broken back. Hell, it was curtains. Busy, or no busy, I went with old pilot Hill into the Ram to heist one for our old pals now gone over a hill — the big one. Heist one, heist two — we held a wake, that's what we did, and ended up at the old corner table, staring red-eyed at that empty chair. A couple of tolerant wives and a worried Mr. Williams broke up the wake before it got fully out of hand — or me fired!

The story of our doings eventually reached the ears of him who enjoyed it most — from Mr. Williams, of course.

"Well, being treated to a wake by two old drinkin' pals is a signal honor, by God . . . and except for weddings and a funeral now and then, neither of them's been inside of a church in twenty years!"

That was a very limited — and nonsensical — side of a near tragedy, but in this not-too-limited view, those two crashes were a turning point from which there was little and only temporary — correction.

Much of the latter part of '55 was spent on "that bloody picture" — in scornful Hemingwayan — a three-way partnership between Papa, Spencer Tracy, and Leland Hayward, as writer, star, and producer, that attempted to produce *The Old Man and the Sea* as a film classic to match the written one. From its beginning in the Cuban locale, a series of bad breaks haunted them — like a couple of hurricanes, for instance. Then efforts for the huge fish the story called for were made off the Peruvian Pacific coast in early '56. Big fish were caught, fourteen feet and over, as I recall

hearing, but none was big enough to satisfy the so-called movie geniuses, who finally resorted to special effects. Speaking of his disgust at the whole business to Taylor early that summer, Papa sort of masked it with a flashback. He said certain things might have gone better if they'd had old Antelope — his and Spencer Tracy's horse — on the crew. "Fishing for a big one from a horse would've made as much sense as some of the stuff we had to put up with, I can tell you that."

Certainly it was a not-too-well Papa who went through the mess. He abhorred the business, but it is quite obvious that he was looking for something and was willing to try.

In the summer of '58 we got a long letter from Miss Mary dated August 13:

It's long after midnight and I have to get up early tomorrow morning, but I can't wait to tell you that just today, Papa decided that we better, pretty soon, get out of this climate for a while and head for Ketchum. We've had it too hot for too long and I feel sure the change will do him good.

We haven't figured out routes or means of transportation, etc., yet; but are sure of two things. We'd appreciate it so much if you could let us know when this year's beast and the bird seasons start — doves, Huns, pheasant, ducks — or whatever you may know about now. If no season opens until, say, the first of Oct., we won't plan to arrive much before that.

Second thing, Papa is deeply involved in a book and he will want a place that is peaceful, quiet — no interrupters, etc., where he can work mornings — shooting in the afternoons or say 3–4 days a week, having fun the other days. There will be just the two of us but, to be comfortable, and give him a decent working space, we ought to have a cabin with two bedrooms — and of course, a view, and a fireplace, and a kitchen decently equipped. I'm going to be the cook, and will hope to find somebody to make beds, clean and wash dishes, if possible. (But that's not so bloody important now.) The important thing is a snug, sweet place for Papa to work and for us to live for, let's say, a couple to four months (quite impossible to be specific about it). I'd like to shoot a deer and eat him; we once went to Italy for two days and stayed nine months; if the weather is lousy consistently, we may pull out.

Bumby, who left Monday for his new office in San Francisco, says Chuck and Floss Atkinson have a fancy new motel, which may be the answer for us — or maybe the old ones on the road to Hailey where we used to stay. (I may have to tote groceries from town on foot, who knows?) Or some completely new place, with space and plenty of daylight, and lamps that can be adjusted for reading at night. A Glamour House with a kitchen, in short.

Dear Fellas, as usual we are imposing on you, asking for this sort of gen. I do hope it's not too much imposition — even now at 1:55 A.M., I'll dream of you and Ketchum all night — no reply was ever waited more fervently.

Scribbled in pencil across the whole letter heading was Papa's short view, angle, whatever:

"DEAR PAPPY AND TILLY: Just read this!" Then he went on to say that his idea was to stay a month and then see — if there was *no publicity* and he wasn't bothered, and if there was shooting, they could stay on. He repeated: Skip ideas of publicity, that he would not have the interrupters that "make it impossible here now!" Certainly it would be wonderful to see us again and he sent his love to Taylor. He would figure out how to hire or buy a car if they came, and: "Tilly, we have a date for the World Series, if you'll go."

I got off a long letter in a hurry; and since I knew that Papa would expect it, I outlined a lot of things local and mentioned changes I knew he wasn't aware of but that

would not affect them in the least — especially in the off-season when Sun Valley closed completely and, miracles of miracles, so did some of the bars in town. Mary's letter indicated they did not know of them, so I reported the addition of that wonderfully sporting game bird now doing very well in our country — the exotic chukar partridge. Not remembering the spook of the old days about rabbits, I mentioned that in the past couple of years we'd been taking the delectable little western cottontails, that we liked better than pheasants — legitimate game animals of the state with a fixed season on them. Hell, I was raised on cottontail rabbits, so why wouldn't I mention them?

Mary's reply was fast, dated August 24, and in the same envelope was a handwritten note from Papa, dated August 26. Mary's letter was a short agreeable one, told me not to overdo it on the house hunting — get something comfortable for a while, then she would house-hunt if they decided to stay. Obviously she'd written it, addressed the envelope, and handed it to Papa for his comments to me in the usual way. I read his note four times, and it took the wind out of my sails. Because of a thing or two about the changes (I'd made my remarks as a joke, more or less to be smart, I suppose) he had thought it all over.

He started off: "Dear Tilly and Dear Pappy: Remember it's been ten years since we were there. . . ." Then he said that if I thought it was so changed that they wouldn't like it anymore I shouldn't be afraid to say so for fear that they might think that they weren't wanted or weren't welcome. Just write frankly! For instance, the fishing in the Gulf Stream was completely changed and almost nonexistent; if anyone wanted to come down for the old fishing they would have to tell them how bad it was. It was simply gone. If Taylor had come down that spring he wouldn't have had any fun. Yesterday there was not a boat out and the town was so changed that an oldtimer wouldn't know it any more. He'd tell anyone truly not to come there. Felt maybe we weren't warning them off because we didn't want to seem inhospitable. They would understand *completely*, and he would truly appreciate it. I should write back as soon as I got this. "Best love, Papa."

In a later conversation Papa said the spooks were pretty much banished, and I should go ahead with arrangements as I saw best. I'd say I almost dropped the phone in relief: I came within a few silly words of lousing up the whole deal. Yes, it had been a long ten years.

7.

The Heiss House Fall

A few minutes before six o'clock the colonel yelled to us in the kitchen: "Here they come, here they come!" His face had been glued to the window for the past half-hour. We rushed in to see a long black Buick station wagon with a white top rolling up the hill, the white-bearded figure pointing to a house that looked familiar to him, and then he saw the figures leaving the window for the front door. The beard parted in a big grin and Bruce swung her around the corner and drew up in a roping-horse stop, doors flying open, arms reaching.

"Aw, gee, we're so ashamed . . . it's been too bloody long!"

The only word to describe the immediate reunion out in the street is: smotherings! And I guess we used more than our side of the street, too. And you knew that when coherence prevailed the bright ones would spring from the bottomless well.

The duck season opened a bit ahead of birds that year, and on our first try at them on Bud's place we got cheated in one choice spot.

Along the bordering hills of the ranch ran an old winding drainage canal several miles long — great for jumping them afoot, its raised outer bank offering concealment in most places, a single lane road atop. We drove over to the canal on a bright Sunday afternoon, and up along it a short way, more or less looking over the situation. Papa drove slowly, reorienting himself, Duke and I the lookouts approaching the bends. On a very wide sweeping one rimming a big bowl in the hills it was a cinch we could put up a healthy rise of mallards. We called a halt, Papa remembered it now, and quiet as mice we loaded guns, got but a few yards from the car on the perfect stalk. Of a sudden,

Papa and hunting pal Bron Zielinski after taking some cottontails.

Right: First loot of the '58 fall.

Overleaf: Hemingway in action.

about two shotgun ranges in distance a swarm of mallards exploded into flight. We straightened up from our crouches at the same instant a stealthy coyote got up off his belly on the low opposite bank of the canal. He just stood there, grinning at us, and trotted off into the low sage, an ear showing now and then, a bushy tail. Mary's rifle was in the car.

"Git the Mannlicher, teach the son of a bitch a lesson . . . even if it is his private domain."

We uncased it in a flash and Mary sent him over the top of that high hill, and he might be going yet by the looks of the bushy appendage propelling him along when we saw him last. Big joke, getting skunked by a

Papa and Bron discussing the Rape of Warsaw.

smart gentleman on a first go-around, and of course the bark of the short-barreled little 6.5 spooked some more farther along, but no matter. We got ducks to hang in the new pantry. Canoes for floating the creek were a thing long since vanished, but "Coyote Bend" would produce again, and other old canals were unchanged, too.

Following the lean postwar waterfowl era, federal law finally reopened the snipe season. They were not plentiful anymore, but in certain short grass meadows in upper Silver Creek you could count on a little shooting in the warm open weather. When Papa, Taylor, and I went to make a precheck of the lower country we got into plenty of them in a couple of places. The colonel, not shooting, climbed a post in a fence corner and marked them down for us, as hawk-eyed as ever. As Papa laughed after many long years away from them, "Well, kid, we had to shoot like hell and depend an awful lot on blind luck to get this many . . . don't tell anyone it was more luck than anything else."

Six of us, Mary and Papa, Taylor and Duke, Till and I, opened pheasant season that fall in Hagerman Valley — the opening barrage on the stroke of noon sounding like El Alamein — walked half the country without filling our limits, and because Papa insisted that rushing icy air was the best cold-preventative, drove the hundred miles home with the windows down like mummies saturated in vodka. Otherwise it was a busy cheerful season with a couple of newcomers joining our mob, making tail-gate and snow-encircled winter picnics, and general fun.

One was Bronislave Zielinski, Papa's Polish translator, who had written that he would be in San Francisco on November 10, with some free days thereafter. Papa organized his flight from the coast to Hailey, our local airport. Between us Papa and I outfitted him with hunting gear, and he turned out to be an excellent wing-shot and a constantly appreciative guest.

Vaulting a fence at Bud Purdy's ranch one day, Papa sprained an ankle, and when we got back to his rented house we called Dr. George Saviers, who stopped by on his way home from the Sun Valley Hospital and diagnosed the ankle as sprained with some damage in heel ligaments. They were instant friends, and remained so for the duration.

8.

New Directions

Our Christmas dinner was a festive occasion with all the trimmings, ala Mary and Tillie. Decorations galore. Papa at his best, joining in the Christmas carols played on our hi-fi a present from the "House of Hemingway." Our little group, the Colonel, Don Anderson, the Duke, Pete and Dorothy Hill from Idaho Falls, friends since 1939. What a Christmas!

The Sunday before New Year's, 1959, Papa said to me, "Well, kid, another one about gone. . . . We'll see a lot of changes in the new one, some we're not looking for, I bet."

It's a cinch that he looked for the one on New Year's — the Castro takeover in Cuba. The apparently calm exterior acceptance of it we did expect because of the long warning. I think I'd have torn my hair out. Phone calls came from a number of outlets wanting the Hemingway view of the

thing as a whole, and we know of only one instance in which he violated his hands-off policy — publicly. Tillie and I walked in when Papa had just hung up the phone on a New York newspaper. We hesitated and began to retreat. Papa grinned, said no, come sit down — we'd seen him in his own doghouse before for saying things he shouldn't have. He finally gave in to Mary's persuasion that he pick up the phone and retract his statement. It was accepted without substitute. Papa admitted breaking his self-rule on the Cuban turmoil, but the retraction brought on a burst of bitterness in which he told us of a nocturnal search of the Finca for excessive, or suspicious, arms by the Guardia Rural of the Batista government. A watchdog was killed by a searcher's rifle butt, and the invasion had prompted Papa to make an official protest. He might as well have tried to spit out the

moon.

In midmonth the Coopers came up for a short stay, about two weeks, the first Idaho reunion in eleven years. Coop was finished with skiing; we had lost them for a number of years earlier in the fifties when they put up a house in Aspen, Colorado; but that honeymoon didn't last long, and they were sort of filtering back to Sun Valley. Coop was due to start a picture in early spring. A first event was a magpie shoot at a private gun club near Bud's place on Silver Creek, followed in about a week with another — the trapping time between. January was its usual stormy self with an above-average fall of snow, so I sneaked off to get in on the fun with both of them, plus a prowling day or two alone with Coop. For some reason Papa didn't go with us. Coop was not a well man, had been under a surgeon's knife, and in his own quiet, indirect way let it be known that he wasn't riding a cloud over the results. But the little time I had with him was as enjoyable as ever.

A significant entry in my January notes concerns a Sunday night, January 18. The colonel was going along fine and we thought it fitting to have a simple dinner at our house, the Hemingways and the Coopers. When I went down to drive Mary and Papa up, the snow was coming down in a solid wall of white. At the table we had the drapes open; the backyard floodlights were on and the world outside was a fairyland. We were "playing the game," which meant digging up old times, and a couple of big fat picture albums came out from the bookshelves base cabinet, the chatter so thick you had a time getting a word in edgewise. Whenever we could, we'd try to maneuver the talk to a favorite listening that we got in snatches from both Mary and Papa — Africa. And of course humor would invariably form the finale. Like the big laughs — with respect attached at Papa having been honored with an "African fiancée" by sage old-timers of a village who

remembered him from the safari back in the thirties. Invariably we'd ask, "Now how old did you say she was, Papa?" He'd howl, look sideways at you, say, "Oh, all of twelve, I'd say, wouldn't you, Kitner?"

And Mary would say, "Judging by her size, I would say about that, and cute, too. Some mighty handsome people over there; you've got to go with your cameras sometime, Pappy."

It was now Papa's habit to take a little lie-down after a good evening meal; Till kept a small car robe on the foot of her bed for him when they came, and when he'd excuse himself the colonel would say, "Well, Chinner's buddy is here tonight, you'll see kitty sneak away from his mat by the fire to join in the siesta. Pappy has to siesta with kitty on the floor, or get his ears pinned back."

"Shhh!" Papa would say. "I'm the best cotsie lawyer in the business, don'tcha know."

The rest of us lingered on at the table and when the records on the hi-fi played out I went in to change them. Sitting cross-legged on the floor facing the bookshelves, half blocking the hall to the bedroom, was Papa, the cat stretched out beside him. "Hell, we got chairs in here, Papa." Oh, this was fine, he said, just reach up to where they were handy — he had books out in little piles, on the floor, the cabinet shelf, amusing himself with old inscriptions in his own stuff, like three cute ones in the six-volume "Sunrise Edition" of 1939:

Earliest Book
by Hemingstein
    X

  his mark   (In Our Time)
Who said this was a dirty book?
Nobody from Glamour House —
(The Harry Morgan Room)
          (To Have and Have Not)
Winner take nothing,
But me Take Tilly
  Hemingstein   (Winner Take Nothing)

Plus a big volume that sold for ten dollars back in 1932 when first published:

> Such a Big Book for Hemingstein to have
> written day and night for such a long long time.
> Hemingstein.   (Death in the Afternoon)

The base cabinet was our "file" of memorabilia of a long, colorful period — our time at Sun Valley, my own then totaling twenty-one years: clippings, magazines, negatives and photographs — all a sort of jumble that would fill a couple of wheelbarrows, but in order that we could thumb to in the dark if need be.

The doors were open, but Papa wouldn't delve into that. He asked me to sit down, he wanted to be sure about the dates of a couple of incidents. He had them right, because I could easily show him, and presently he said, "With all the 'bait' you and Till have kept so intact you ought to do a history of your time here . . . hell, you grew up with Sun Valley, came before it was fully born, helped in a bigger way than you may realize to make it what it is. . . ."

"And to change a lot of things that we don't like today, Papa," I cut in.

"That's a part of it, always in such cases," he said matter-of-factly. "But it's been lots of fun for you, so I meant what I said."

"If I felt that I was good enough to do it, Papa, I'd be inclined to try and vanish somewhere . . . it wouldn't be history of the kind we read in school, you know."

"No, it sure as hell wouldn't." He laughed. "You might feel safe on the moon, say."

"If I ever do try it, Papa." — I laughed, for that was my angle of thought — "shall I include you in?"

"Oh." He grinned. "I guess we could look into the mirror and maybe scratch it a little, but I don't think we'd break it."

We were joined when things were cleaned up in the kitchen. Even the colonel overdid himself and didn't ask to be taken home before his dinner was settled. The last music on the hi-fi that night was the only kind that he ever stated a special liking for: Stephen Foster favorites, sung by the Old Groaner himself, Bing Crosby, whom we both knew slightly from earlier days when his boys spent the summers here. We took the total party home around eleven o'clock, blinded by the snow but making it easy with chains on, the new fall up to the car door bottoms. While all this was going on, down Hollywood way in California, a needless, senseless thing took place that would change a few things for Till and me.

Early Monday morning I got a business call from our Los Angeles public relations office, a routine thing about pictures I had in the works for them, then the shocking news and a tip-off. Over a minor domestic spat in his home that didn't amount to a hill of beans, publicity chief Vince Hunter's first cameraman had locked himself in the bathroom, put the muzzle of an automatic pistol in his ear, and pulled the trigger. The tip-off was that Vince would call me within the hour and was ready to catch the afternoon train for a talk with me about taking the job. The interim gave me time to think out any number of angles, the background of the situation, and try to understand. I knew the man well as we had worked together on occasion, including a solid winter in the filming of a difficult ski movie for Sun Valley promotion but a few seasons before. He was good at his work. We were not close friends, but there was much in common; thus it did not set well with me to take on a fine job from the wreckage. The other view was that I wanted to broaden my scope, Vince had taken on a raw apprentice to learn the business, and now he found himself ready to go full-out on several major films — a program stretching ahead indefinitely. I told Vince to catch the train.

We spent a full day together. The

immediate prospects of the job were even more attractive than I had thought, and I had a week to think it over after Vince left; he would call me then. We thought it best to make a definite yes or no of our own before talking to anyone. It was, of course, yes, and I called the Hemingways. The man of the house happened to answer, said, "Sure thing, Mr. Pappy, come on down. Hope it's good. I saw down at the magpie shoot the other day that something was on your mind."

Till and I went down after work and my opener was this: "Papa, Vince Hunter was up from California, spent a day with us, and —"

"He isn't going to take you away from us, is he?" he cut in on me, not alarmed, but keenly tuned, wanting the works. I outlined it in full, the four of us perched on the counter stools, and I can't remember a better audience for a ten-minute, uninterrupted spiel; the good side of it making the warm response, the from-the-hearts blessings. Indulge me in a brief necessary sketch of it:

Around March 1 I would go to Hollywood for a period of road and studio production work, and return to Idaho coincidentally with the opening of the agricultural season — May, roughly — with two full-length railroad traffic promotional films to make involving irrigation, potatoes (the major industry in Idaho), and relevant activities. My working territory would be immense, but a commonly conceded fact in railroad talk was (and is) the "breadbasket division" for origin of freight revenue was the Idaho division. Thus it was almost certain that as a matter of convenience all around my working base for at least two years ahead would be our home, where I would stop off most weekends, traveling from there to different areas. There was a vague possibility of a change of plans, but this was not likely once I started on the program. I was cautioned, however, to keep a residential move in mind, and be prepared

for it. The advantages of the whole far outweighed the disadvantages. Right or wrong, the decision was ours — a quote from my audience when the picture was clear, and with us, he was convinced that it was the right one. Papa did say, "Miss Mary and I could cry with the thought of you two moving from here . . . but we won't think of it in that light. It's the line in your work that you like best and you've gone the distance where you are, don't know how you've stood it lately, from what I know."

He naturally asked how it all came about so suddenly and I told him exactly how it was, had with me the Los Angeles paper carrying the story (the suicide means the same as his father's had been), and that bothered me, but I had no other choice — news reaches everywhere. He didn't bat an eye, or change expression, but said, "Happenstance, true, but at an odd time, things changing so fast we can't keep up with them."

Our talk was no more than an hour, and we were especially taken with Papa's "You've been on one track a long time but you're adaptable, kid. We've seen the evidence, you know."

I wondered about that — I was "coming on fifty-three," not exactly a pup anymore.

Our next tough facing was the colonel, and we did ask advice about waiting until after his birthday party coming up February 6 — his seventy-second. We knew that he would bluster like a hen searching out a fence hole, but that his blessings were a cinch in due time. We'd wait, and tell him we'd have cocktail hour and dinner most weekends and that Miss Till would be training someone for her job through the coming summer and to the resort's fall closing (that was all set). I began at once getting my loose ends picked up, my next-in-line ready to take over.

The colonel's birthday party was at Clara Spiegel's, a small group that year, but a perfect gem. His cakes always were gems,

With some Idaho friends.

too, Sun Valley's head baker knowing him
well, outdoing our suggestions with little
touches of his own — for that one, tiny,
perfectly done bear tracks meandering
between tiny pines, a blue sugar trout
stream, small bits of something for sage, the
trail so for-real that you looked for the little
chocolate bruin that made it. Words are

beyond me for the feeling at Taylor's anniversaries. His "boys," Duke and Don, had duty call after the preliminaries, so for the dinner there were the Hemingways, Doc and Pat Saviers, the hostess and her neighbors across the street — and the neighbor's camera and a pocketful of flashbulbs. Probably the toast that warmed the colonel's gay spirits the most was Papa's to their twentieth anniversary as friends. On so many of his facets that evening Taylor was as much like the fifty-two of those long-ago days as we'd seen for some time.

Twelve days later, our old friend was gone.

The fatal blow struck on Tuesday morning, the seventeenth, after we'd had breakfast with him at the staff tables. He was joking good with a couple of ski instructors, jawing about it being a gray gloomy day outside. It would be chilly in the trees along the river at the foot of the ski lift. The sunshine was always welcome there — sharpened a fellow, helped him watch for the chiselers with the phony ski-lift tickets — "the goddamn cheapskates, anyhow!" He waved to me from the path to the Ski School meeting place about nine, as I worked at my desk by the window; his head was pulled into his turned-up collar, and I felt a tinge of something I couldn't call guilt when I thought of how great he'd been at our house the previous Saturday night, putting his good sign on our future. I sat there pondering it a few minutes, then suddenly Tillie yelled at me from out front to come quick. I was at the door in nothing flat to see an employee and a guest practically carrying Taylor Williams between them as they turned toward our shop.

The poor man was in agony, scarcely able to speak, hands at his chest, sounding like a man half drowned. Somehow I knew that it wasn't what we feared when we set him down at my desk where he couldn't hold up his head. Till had the ambulance there in no time and I waited at the hospital for a word on what to do. I got it in minutes

from Doc Saviers: see if I could locate Taylor's son Bob in Portland, Oregon — advise him to catch the first train if he was in port. Fortunately, he was, heading for sea within a day or two. Then I headed for the Hemingways', but George Saviers' call beat me there — which helped a little. By four that afternoon when Papa and I spoke a few words to the colonel, he recognized us in his sedation, squeezed our hands, and wondered what the hell it was that knocked him down in the snow. Doc said he had a clue to what the trouble was.

At ten that night I looked in on him — sound asleep. I saw Papa in the Lodge lobby at eleven; he'd had a very few words with the colonel, he said, but he never told me what they were. He was waiting for a taxi to take him home and talked but a minute outside. For once in my time I saw Papa Hemingway hard put for words. Among the few spoken: "I'm afraid that it isn't any good, Mr. Pappy."

The colonel passed on at 1:00 A.M., and while we were at breakfast Doc Saviers called to ask that I try to contact Bob's train en route. I talked to him by company telephone at an Oregon division stop, got his ready okay for the autopsy Doc asked for. His findings proved his hunch: an atrophied (thinned with age) stomach wall had ruptured upward, penetrating the lung cavity — very rare in medical history, it was said.

"But leave it to Taylor to do it a little different than we ordinary folks," Doc added.

"Yes," Bob said. "It's like Dad, all right."

It reminded me of a typical remark of Taylor's back in 1952 when we attended the funeral of a friend, a popular ski instructor killed in an avalanche. The snow was seven feet deep on the valley floor and the looping one-lane access road in the cemetery was opened by Sun Valley's big rotary plow; the grave, like all done even in average winters, opened right beside the half-walled swath.

"Finest country in the world to live in," Taylor said to me. "But it's hell to have to be buried in it in winter."

On the phone Bob had told me to go ahead with whatever arrangements I could. The five-foot level of snow was the first problem. I felt it proper that the colonel's resting place be as near Gene Van Guilder's grave as we could get it — some sixty feet from the road, all by itself for all of those years. I learned while Bob was en route that plenty of available space was there. When I told Papa, he said, "Gee, kid, I was hoping that you would propose that, because it's not for me to suggest."

"Why not, Papa? Bob considers us as much family around his father as himself. . . ."

"Yes, I'm quite sure that he does. I remember him well, and I know he'll approve . . . but it will take a shovel brigade, a small army, to move that much snow out to Gene's; I was out that way not long ago and from the highway I noticed that you can't see even a hump in the snow where the lilac bushes are on his grave."

I guess my one "sin" while in service to the town was in borrowing its equipment to take the place of a shovel gang. We had recently purchased a Michigan loader, a versatile affair for cleaning out intersections following the regular plow; and my good friend and town marshal, Les Jankow, was glad to bring it out when the Valley sent down its rotary to open the long U-shaped loop of the little cemetery's road. The once shabby burial ground was now a credit to the community, due to voluntary citizens' action in cleaning it up: a carpet of fine grass, an irrigating system, and caretaker — paid for by a tax levy. But opening a grave well out from easy access had never been done with a machine. The man handling the sale of the twenty-five-dollar plots buckled on his high overshoes to come along with his map for recording, quite vexed at our insistence on that one spot. Ours was quite the operation on the bright,

snappy day, the snow a bit deeper than we thought, due to the sharply rising hill that piled it there on the lee side of the prevailing storm direction. As I was the only skiing man, I put on my skis and probed for what seemed eternity because we got slightly off the "key," which was one of two small footstones, right beside the rotary's cut. Papa had insisted on coming along to help in any way that he could, and he was one of the guiding-eye sidewalk superintendents, standing on the high fat tires of the stubby Michigan machine. When my long shovel handle finally hit the low stone wall about Gene's grave my hands and my feet were about to fall off. The snowfield looked like a cribbage board. Then the big rotary came in on an angle to miss the footstones (the operator could run it along a silk-walled tent and not touch a thread), backed out for Les to open a high-banked clearing. It wasn't pretty, by any standards, but the turn-on-a-dime Michigan did the job in no time and high-heeled ladies' pumps could get to the gravesite without much discomfort on the slumbering green grass practically free of snow. I got a welcome nip from a brandy flask, the town got back its gasoline.

Bob's selection of pallbearers included an earliest Idaho neighbor of his father, Mr. Hicks, in charge of Sun Valley motor transportation; old guide Jack Redden; George Saviers; Forrest MacMullen; myself; and Ernest Hemingway — listed last because in his humility he thought that he intruded over much older friends like retired Pop Mark and much-liked old-time neighbor, Dan Knight. Old guide Art Wood could not make it, and Don Anderson, who had once roomed with Taylor, emotionally asked to be excused.

We buried the colonel on Saturday afternoon, February 21, a bright, almost balmy day in which our jackets were warm enough. As he was so different in life, Taylor's simple service had a touch of difference, too. As long as we knew him,

125

God's great out-of-doors was his church, and the young minister was a newcomer, his subject a stranger to him. Undertaker Ray McGoldrick, of Hailey, called me over to the Opera House a bit ahead of the service, and to my surprise our neighbor a block down the hill in town waited for me — a sheaf of sheet music on her arm. I'd known Frances Campbell since I'd come to Idaho and hadn't the foggiest notion that she was an organist. Bob was not there yet, so she asked my opinion on her music. It came so fast for me, I guess, that I said something like "Gosh, Franny, I don't know . . . the only music I ever knew Taylor had preference for is Stephen Foster's, and I guess that would hardly . . . or would it?"

I guess that as well as she knew him, too, she had something similar in mind, for she only smiled and turned to go to the Hammond organ. I had to smile to myself, too, in suddenly recalling that back in my professional days we always liked to be able to say of funeral music, "Fore and aft, no vocals, thank God!" I was thinking it then for the colonel. For the attendance file-in, Franny's soft, perfectly tempoed old folksy ballad, "Red River Valley," was exactly right; I, for one, felt the colonel's presence beside me, as I think each soul in the house did. The young minister had a bit of a time of it, and you felt for him, as I felt a squirm a time or two in the big frame next to me in our row.

At the conclusion of the service, Frances turned to the favorite composer, and I don't believe that I've ever heard "My Old Kentucky Home" so beautifully played. As we pallbearers waited at the side door there was not a murmur from any of us, but as the casket was wheeled between us, I felt a tickle of whiskers on my ear, and turned to the soft whisper: "The sermon a bit off for the colonel . . . but the lady on that organ, we owe her a rare gold coin."

Very shortly afterward the date for my departure was set as March 8; I was pretty

126

much in the clear, so I coasted along. Within himself, Papa cried at our loss, but only one time did I hear him voice it — an evening at our house. We stood looking out the window, a serene hour in the mountains when above the deep-shadowed slopes the alpenglow colors a high one here and there. He said that he hated the thought of Miss Till rattling around in the house all by herself, even if it would only be for a couple of months. Then: "Well, Mr. Pappy, it hurts when your old friends die off, and you can't dodge it that as you go along, some move away . . . we've lost a few in our time . . . we lost Gene in the worst hard luck, we lost Bud Hegstrom when he moved away while we were away so long, and now we've lost the colonel . . . with you two, he was of the beginning out here . . ."

He broke it off suddenly, apologized for "poking the gloom spook," but asked that as I went along on the new work during the summer and gained an idea of the foreseeable future, I let them know. I promised. In the interim the subject of a house that I had photographed came up again. I obtained the keys from a local who looked after it, let it be known that I had them, suggesting to Papa that if he was interested after he saw it, he talk to Chuck Atkinson who'd have an idea of price due to his business connections with the local lawyer for whom I'd done the picture job. He said he might. That was on Saturday, March 7, when Till and I spent the afternoon and evening at the Hemingways, loafing, talking, having a good time a week ahead of the Hemingways' departure, their lease up on March 15. I took down a number of small photographs that I'd made, to be inscribed and mailed to Hemingway friends everywhere — that little act no less than a circus.

From the Lodge at noon on Sunday I left on the bus for my train. When Papa embraced me in his usual way for such occasions and said: "Give Coop a ring when you get in down there," I had a bit of a time answering him. I gave Tillie the keys that I had and Papa told me they would look at the house with Chuck during the coming week.

For the drive to Key West Papa rented a Hertz car. The route was by way of Las Vegas, across Arizona and Texas to New Orleans.

About the same time they departed Las Vegas, Chuck Atkinson and George Kneeland, the local lawyer, left Phoenix, where they had played a little golf with Bob Topping, the owner of the house and acreage around it on the west bank of Big Wood River a short way north of Ketchum. Bob built the house back in the early fifties when he married a local girl, an ice-skating employee at Sun Valley; lived in it a few years and quit Idaho for an easier climate. The house was furnished, ready for occupancy — then.

The two parties met about halfway — at Kingman, Arizona — stopped for a talk, then went on their ways. A short time into April, Chuck got through to the Finca by phone. Papa told him that he'd put a check for the house into the mail to him that day. Then Chuck mentioned that a Hailey merchant had a claim against certain small items like dishes, a few portable appliances and the like, and that he'd been instructed to allow their pickup by the claimant. Oh, hell, that stuff did not amount to anything, Papa said, but don't let them cart away that big stock of several thousand clay targets stacked in the basement garage (true, Topping dallied in trapshooting, had a regulation trap installed on the downriver flat near the main entrance gate to the property).

So, the Hemingway Idaho "hunting lodge" — "chalet" — "retreat" — what have you, came into being. In truth it was a fine home, for part-time or permanent living, its interior arrangement ideal for two people like the Hemingways. On the outside the house was not so pretty: cast in solid concrete, a borrow from the construction method used on Sun Valley's Lodge to almost exactly duplicate roughhewn timber walls; the concrete was not yet stained in autumn brown, imparting the weathered look; the house was a two-story square with a hip roof that made it resemble "a blockhouse, a Fort Dearborn, like the pictures in our history books in school." It was built to last indefinitely, however, its inside a classic in lovely wood paneling throughout, huge double-glazed windows bringing outdoors inside, the river sparkling along below, a hundred yards out from the broad sun deck along the east-fronting forty-foot-long living room. Some of the furnishings were a bit on the bizarre side, however, and not exactly to tastes of the new owners — which I damn well knew long before. To use a quote, they gave it a sort of "vulgar" look. The first thing Chuck had done was stain the exterior walls, making it a different house altogether to the eye.

In my short seven weeks in California I was on the road a great deal with Vince, working on two films of the state. Ready to head north on April 20, I got Mary's long letter — a carbon copy of her original to Till in Ketchum. Its surprises were reason for me to read it, I think several times at least, on the way to San Francisco.

The first one was typed above the letterhead: "Our European address to be used from now on: Care Guaranty Trust Co. of New York — Place de la Concorde, Paris."

I recalled not even so much as a hint of a European summer, and one paragraph convinced me that their route home might have inspired thoughts of Spain in Papa's head. A wonderfully newsy letter, too.

Your fine letter, Pappy, about the job and your whereabouts, the good news that you'll be working in Idaho this summer came just this morning and I want to answer it quick before we get into the final whirligig of packing. I slipped a carbon in, so you don't have to forward or quote from this wacky

epistle. Before anything else, Till darling, that was the cutest birthday card I've ever had [description for me in parentheses, their birthdays a "thing" between them, just one day apart] — so gay you must have designed it yourself, had it custom made. My birthday was fine — it was a wild day on the "oceany" and after so long away from it, we had to work to keep our balance; but the sun was bright and the breeze perfumed and sweet, and Gregorio made fish with a favorite green sauce for lunch, and the sea produced a small present — one shining green and blue and gold dorado. How sweet the boys [Duke and Don] were to give you a shirt, Till.

Looking back on it, seems to me we were all stirred up emotionally for quite a while this year, with Taylor and then Pappy's leave-taking — that last night at our place was the kissingest and huggingest session I can recall ever. We were still limp and exhausted when we got to Elko, and Dan Bilbao and his wife gave us a fine time and a fine dinner and I was too tired to appreciate.

But in general our trip down was just great — gay and lucky too — no snowstorms, no rain, only very strong winds. Total mileage, 4,091.9 — of which we spent 1,156.6 in Texas alone. Went across the Rio Grande first at El Paso, to Juarez on Palm Sunday — nice town without much character; next at Eagle Pass to Piedras Negras which is an adorable town with charming people, a gay, sparkling center square, fine market, pretty baroque church; finally at Laredo, with Nuevo Laredo dusty and hot and unattractive. Papa had a great reunion with Waldo Pierce, the artist, in Tucson and I fell in love with him — he's a true genius, with the sparkliest, gayest, widest-ranging enchanting mind we've met in a long time (awfully nice, pleasant wife) and a down-east accent, had me translating, as from a foreign language for the first hour.

We left Hotch at the airport in New Orleans to fly to the coast and came on in fine style, Papa driving very well and my nerves — you know how active they are in cars — gradually calming down. We saw the second half of FWTBT in Phoenix and I was moved to great admiration for Hotch's script and the directing and acting. Papa not wholly in favor — but largely so — his criticisms, of course, very acute.

Good news here, we had the usual blood tests etc. And Papa's things are all good, ie. all negative, which is just great. And my blood count up to over four million for the first time in years. Oh, Idaho! Other good news —the Finca is just lovely — scores of flowering trees and vines and shrubs — the planting around the pool lusher than ever and the pool divine, just cool enough to be stimulating and the water sparkling blue.

Pappy darling, I haven't answered your letter at all; but you know we're both delighted and excited that things are working out so well for you. It's rough on Till now but we have great faith in her capacity to survive rough stuff and you have the summer to look forward to, so we take off feeling just fine about you two.

We go to N.Y. next week (CONFIDENTIAL) *and sail for Algeciras, Spain (confidential). Papa told me to take my fur coat, so who knows when we'll be back, either here or Idaho. But it wouldn't surprise me if we leave Europe before fur coat weather and turn up in Ketchum for at least part of the bird season. But we'll keep in touch. Dearest fellas — the greatest of luck to youse and the jobs and the house — and your healths — and also funwise."*

Love and kisses — MARY

Scrawled across the bottom of Till's original:

Best love, SIR TILL *— I miss you very much — hope everything going okay.*

PAPA

The "Sir Till" was the result of a "knighting" for something she did that for the life of us we can't remember; but we do recall the ceremony, the flat of a butcher knife blade on her head at the Hemingways one night. One thing she did not forget occurred during the week after I left. Down at the house that evening, all the change got to her; butterflies in her stomach, losing the bit of food she tried to eat. Papa drove her home and walked back. Early the next morning she heard him calling from out in the backyard where he could see her upstairs window. He hadn't used the phone since ours was downstairs, and he feared she was too ill to answer it. She assured him she was much better and asked him in for coffee; no, he just wanted to be sure — thought she might need a doctor. A day or two into the following week the telephone man came and installed an upstairs extension. Pretty thoughtful, that, for a gal alone who would often be called at night, by me; and the instrument matched the color scheme of the room. 'Nuf said.

Back home in Idaho on April 30, I hit the road at once — the program working out almost exactly as planned. A first direct word was from Mary, dated June 7, Malaga, Spain. It seemed they were headquartering at the palatial home of an old friend, Bill Davis, her list of familiar place names to be taken in for the bullfights indicating that the summer over there was only a pup! Instinct said it was a binge in preparation — surprising, considering the austerity theme we knew, and yet it was not. In her note was the first mention of the Topping house, confirming certain matters I'd warned about, she not getting anywhere in having a few interior changes made through the offers of Chuck to oversee.

One weekend in early July I bumped into George Saviers and was delighted to hear that he and Pat were going on a vacation to Spain right away, would meet up with the Papa entourage. It instantly struck me that it was his birthday month — they might run into a party. George said they just might, at that. The sixtieth year seems to be significant, observation of others told me. They ran into the party, indeed, and we got Mary's mailed description of it while it was tapering off the following evening of July 22 — at the Davis home in Malaga. Well and good, but it had a purpose, her build-up to the true point:

". . . a crazy letter, but had to get this off my chest before I try to get down to business. No room in this zany life we lead of constant celebrations, and I'm getting awfully hungry for a day Papa and I might share, with absolutely nobody else at all around."

My busy summer naturally required above-normal concentration, but I had lots of time to think on long drives to and from distant work areas. Sensitive to a fault, perhaps, I often felt guilt probing the reasons that were "none of your damn business, tend to your own knitting, for what can you do about it, anyway?" But after all, it was my business, and I had stuck my nose into it before — voluntarily and by request — and how else would I know a little of what was going on a continent and an ocean away? So often I would think of that long-ago time when Papa showed me the source — John Donne's writing — of his title for FWTBT, and when I'd read it, he said, "Christ, if a man could write like that!"

He made quite a thing of it, was especially attracted by the lines:

Any man's death diminishes me, because I am involved in Mankinde; And therefore never send to know for whom the bell tolls; it tolls for thee.

For I finally had to come clean with myself, as I finally have to do here: I was intensely worried about my friend, and I had been for a long time. Somehow, to me, it was man's business, I'd even be reluctant to speak about it at home. As to doubt in my mind as to what was happening to Papa's, there was none whatsoever. You can walk through thick timber and all trees have a

tendency to look alike, but a big one — a great one — stands out from the others, a thing apart, calling attention to itself; and when you don't live in the timber, but observe it from a middle distance, liking the tree for what it is and not its name over a long period of time, you hardly can fail to come up with a fairly good image on the ground glass of overall perspective. True, for ten years I had observed through the eyes and ears of another. But the second hand, I was quite sure, had prepared me for the introduction to the image that alarmed me — the first glimpse of it in a handwritten letter. I said that it took the wind out of my sails. It did, but the great '58 fall brightened the picture so much that at times you just knew it was the old days coming back. In the background, of course, was the mounting Cuban thing; a waiting trigger, and when tripped, the process, the turmoil within, came to the surface in all too frequent intervals throughout the winter of '59. It was, quote not mine, a "problem winter."

Yet, as the summer advanced, there came some brightening signs: Chuck commenced to receive interior things for the house from Spain, requests to have a few major changes made. In early September when I was in town he showed me what he'd had done to the long living room, and I hardly knew it. Gone was the glaring red wall-to-wall carpet, in its place, warm-colored tile; the big distasteful bar, looking like a refined hogshead, was gone from one outside corner opposite the stairs. The one room alone made it a different house inside, so you could speculate that perhaps Mary was right about no fur-coat weather in Spain — even a guy who'd only read about them knew that they couldn't fight bulls all winter!

I kept a promise when my summer work was finished and my fall program was slowed a bit before the bustling far-flung harvests. In a meeting with him on further increases in my schedule, the boss flatly told me that I could forget any possibility of having to change place of residence for a very long time. I at once fired away an airmail letter to the Paris address, and we heard no more until one October weekend when I stopped at home but a few hours. Tillie had received two identical color postcards, addressed and written to her, of the ship, *Liberte*, that brought Papa home from Europe. Both said he was lonely, for there was no one aboard he knew; both mentioned a "secret" of his and Till's of the previous fall; both were written in mid-Atlantic, and mailed together in New York two days hence. We could not know why he was all by himself, or what was going on, and what was coming up. I drove way down into Colorado that trip, and I'm not a bit certain of remembering any other than a deep and sickening feeling much of the way.

I finished my outside work in early November and scheduled my vacation for the balance of the month. Tillie had her replacement trained by then and we took a long week to fly with Pete and Dorothy Hill to New Orleans — his a business trip, with time for all of us to have fun. We checked in at the Hotel Monteleone a bit past noon on Sunday, November 15, and landed back at Idaho Falls on Monday, November 23. Resting after lunch, we made a Christmas date with the Hills, leaving it open as to where — their house or ours — depending. We drove into Ketchum about six o'clock, me with a quick errand to run. Back shortly, I found Tillie on the phone with Mary Hemingway. They'd been back but a few days, had a date for the evening; there was plenty of time, though, so run out and say hello. Tillie had enough so that on our way out she gave me a fair sketch.

Mary had flown back from Europe in October to organize at the Finca, Papa came by boat — as per his postcards. While they were in Cuba, the great Spanish matador, Antonio Ordonez, with a Mexican itinerary

ahead of him, stopped by with his pretty wife, Carmen. Papa talked the bullfighter into coming out to Idaho for some hunting. They got in a little, then a sudden change in the Ordonez plans were sending them on their way to Mexico the following day. Papa was quite upset about it, she said. Mary had flown up to Chicago to shop for some essentials for the house, then flew on out while the others came by car — Roberto Herrara, the chauffeur.

Roberto met us at the front door, Mary on the run behind him. Volubly glad to see us, she looked a bit fagged, too. Which she promptly said that she was — having to feed her visitors on paper plates before her dishes came from Chicago!

"Never a dull moment, you know, I hardly knew my way about the house — couldn't remember it."

As we chatted there by the step up into the hall, Papa's back was to us as he talked with the handsome couple by the fireplace — totally unaware of our arrival. Over his shoulder I saw Ordonez's eyes shift from his toward us, his head nodding. Papa went on talking, palms upward in the familiar emphasis spread. Mary took over, our chatter increasing as we approached.

"Hi, Miss Till, Mr. Pappy. Heard you went to New Orleans, thought you never would get back."

He graciously introduced us to the couple, made a clever, amusing production of the seesaw translations about given names — right in the old groove — then abruptly reverted to all-out Spanish in taking on the one-sided intent conversation. I was surprised that neither of the couple spoke much English — our impression, anyway. Then we eased away toward the kitchen to pour a short one and do a fast shakedown with Mary and Roberto — and to know the pleasant dusky Jamaican girl, Lola, whom Mary flew out from the Finca with her, and whose full British accent made this mountain boy say to himself: Well, ah'll be damned!

Dr. George Saviers, Bron Zielinski, Papa, and rancher John Powell

With an eye on the time, we eased back to the living room, our coats on, my hat in hand. Rather abruptly, the Ordonez couple offered their excuses to go upstairs to change, and he spoke our names perfectly. I don't believe it was my imagination that saw a faint shrug of his shoulders, an accompanying slight cock of his head, as if

Ordonez conveyed his: Sorry, I guess you can see how it is. Nor can I recall a more awkward minute or so, after their leave-taking, than trying to find something to say or do while a lonely Papa stared silently down into the fireplace, fingers hovering about his lower lip.

Suddenly he was back to reality, radiant as molten metal. He folded Sir Till in his arms, asked his first question: "Where did you stay in New Orleans?"

"At the Monteleone, Papa . . . had a great time, too."

His surprise widened his eyes, split his beard, then it all froze.

"What day did you get in down there?"

She told him and he said, "Well, I'll be damned, we waited for Carmen to come from church, got a late start, checked out about an hour before you came . . . what a shame that we didn't let you know, and you might have come a day early. . . ."

Did we get into the Famous Door on Bourbon Street, hear Al Hirt split that trumpet, did we eat at the Vieux Carre — and so on? Yes, we probably got into too many doors on old Bourbon Street, and we had a couple of good stories, but we had to go — and we did not want to leave because it was going good. Mary said that she would call us tomorrow and Papa came outside with us, down the steps to our car. He was forthright and open about the disappointment of his friends leaving so suddenly, without notice; said that he didn't mind the dough he spent gearing them up, just thought that we could all have a fine time, a few more days; he could spare the time from going to work — the stuff he'd gathered over there during the summer.

"And don't you think they're really fine people?"

His "going to work" was an opening, so I hinted that it wouldn't do to try to jack up the fine big walnut dresser in his room, scar up its top with a makeshift where he could write. No, he guessed it wouldn't but it was a fine place to write, that big window

looking up the river, the Boulder Mountains for a background. I didn't merely offer — I said right out that with lumber scraps I had, I'd make a hightopped stand for him, do it tomorrow, and it wouldn't be very pretty, made in a hurry.

"Pretty don't write." He grinned. "As I was once told."

"Yeah, I know," I said. "But I can't remember her name."

"The hell you can't." He laughed. "And say, there are a few northern ducks down. . . ."

"I'm behind in that work, Papa. Long gun or short one?"

"Oh, they're a little wild, and so what?"

The evening air was right nippy, and as we drove out the main gate a couple of hundred yards from the house, my rear-view mirror showed him silhouetted in the wide front door, just standing there in his shirt sleeves. Physically, Papa looked fine, and he *was* himself in the last ten minutes or so that we were there; but there is only one word for that other: obsession — and we wondered what he'd been searching for all summer. Certainly it was an old well-worn subject — as to "the stuff" that he said he'd gathered.

Entirely from scraps and plenty of tools in my basement shop, I whipped together an old-fashioned bookkeeper's affair that would do the job very well, and we took it out to the house in midafternoon. We shoved the heavy dresser to one side in the tasteful "man's" bedroom so beautifully paneled in solid walnut. I was ashamed of the scrubby thing we marred it with, and said so.

"Yeah, a hog in a parlor," was his hearty, laughing response. "But I tell you, kid, I'll boot a hog in the butt if we haven't done worse in our time."

The day was the indescribable kind that makes the mountain country falls what they are — good to be alive, wrapped in something that you vow you'll never allow to escape you. Down in the sun-flooded kitchen our gals were at it like farm wives catching up on the doings — "any takers, gentlemen, we're not budging for a while." You bet, there were takers — the time was exactly right for talk. I think we expected a "confession" report of the summer, and we got it — straight, all-out, told with laughs, as good as if you were there, and "it wasn't exactly what you'd call tourist class, I can tell you that, kids!"

It was the perfect time for a bit of kidding, which I did by taking up the indifference over essentials claimed, but concern over the stock of clay targets in the basement.

"Yes, fine thing." Mary laughed. "To hell with what the housekeeping department has to do with, just so there's essentials for shooting." Sure, you're damned right, gotta have those — and the place would've been a better bargain with a handtrap thrown in — good place straight out from the back door where the drive curves up the hill, good background, over the trees along the winding river to the north — a low rail fence to set your stack of targets and shells on. How much vacation time did I have left? A week, too broke for anything but hunting ducks; then a trip to California for reviewing work, then back on December 7 — for certain. Did I have absolute faith in the no-moving business?

"Absolutely, Papa. I'm halfway through two films, and I'm slated for all winter right here in Idaho, filming in processing plants, glorifying the lowly potato, home weekends, and did you get my letter about it?"

Yes, but they couldn't remember where they were, and the best news, ever: "A gone spook that's bothered us since back in the spring. And did you get home for your birthday, kid?"

Yes, I had, close to home, made it on the nose, a Friday night, and we just finished celebrating it, and other things.

"Well, that makes us even then." He grinned.

Tillie and I subtly fished for an idea of

how long in the West this time — a futile fishing — and dodged by a little rundown that indicated it wasn't so bad in Cuba. Dodged again by reminding Sir Till that she had a New Orleans story or two. She did, a fitting one, a smash hit: It was cold at night, and on one of them we had waited for our friends to finish business — in a Bourbon Street bar where a top-billing stripper playing to an early scant house bought us two hillbilly kids a drink (which hit you $3.00 per round). Probably a part of her act, and so what; but the kick was the between-acts come-on gal, dressed in a powder puff and goose pimples due to the barker holding open the front door for passersby to get a peek of the raw inside. We sat at the bar, our backs to the door, and I could reach out and almost touch the goose pimples. Tillie showed her sympathy and the gal said, "Yes, ma'am, it's cold, and I hope the suckers get out and in quick so loud-mouth there can shut that goddamn door!"

"A fine story, Miss Till . . . it rhymes perfectly with 'roll up that goddamn window!' "

"On one leg of our flight down we flew over the Oklahoma-Texas panhandle country, and Pete edged over a few miles so that I could get a good look at my grandfather's old ranch. I hadn't seen it in forty years, but I recognized it miles away by the durable old white gypsum stone house that stuck out like a sore thumb, in country changed so much that I wouldn't have known it otherwise — except for certain scattered features. I was the kid all over again, open-mouthed, as Pete did me a circle, everyone amused, which I doubt I heard."

"And why not?" Papa said as warmly as if it had been he. "Those things nothing can ever take from you. That part of Pappy's young life I always envied . . . imagine me having such fun if after forty years I was flown over Oak Park, Illinois . . . Michigan, yes, the part I know."

Though he was casual about it, Papa was pleased with the few changes made since they had been only lukewarm at the first look at the house. They had "borrowed back" the two cotsies from our neighbors who kept them; the hides were scattered about as throw rugs; the gun rack in the living room corner by the front hall step "makes it even smell like you guys, the gun oil, and leather," as I put it. Papa laughed.

"I hope so. When we first looked in that room I thought we were in the Western branch of the old Everleigh Sisters' Club in Chicago . . . only I wasn't that old in those days."

Mary wanted another change made; in a couple of big upholstered pieces: remove the bulging "bosoms" of the back cushions. Hell, they were all right — that kind of work cost a little dough! He lost that round — to a female army of two, and Mary teased him: "We don't mind a little extravagance — just on occasions, do we, lamb?"

"Naw, Kitner . . . I guess we don't, at that."

As a bonus? She got a hi-fi set, too, installed in a high-vertical antique cabinet that she found in Spain and shipped it well ahead. Of course that might have evened the score — the fine swivel-mounted TV sets in the house were a must for the weekly prizefight shows — to one who also loved good music.

We rustled about and borrowed a handtrap to do the first backyard trapshooting on Thanksgiving afternoon; shot well into dusk, wearing yellow glasses for contrast, the muzzles of our guns stabbing the gloom with pencils of flame; an old "shooting machine" breaking them neat as ever out over bare cottonwood limbs, good for judging the range. On Friday, Roberto returned to Cuba, and I stayed home from a duck hunt, to do a few things ahead of our trip. Bad luck hit hard.

On a stalk, a hidden snaky willow root on rough ground tripped Mary for a nasty fall. She obeyed the first law of the hunter — save your precious weapon first. She did, taking the jolt on her left elbow, going down so fast that she could not straighten out to take it with her hand. It was a bone-shattering, excruciatingly painful break. George Saviers was along, saw the gravity of it at once. They broke all records for the Sun Valley hospital. At the house that evening he had no choice but to say that it was like putting together a crushed eggshell, and that it would be touch-and-go to bring Mary out of it with a bendable elbow — even partially so. We saw her a few minutes Saturday afternoon, in a cumbersome boomerang-shaped cast, gritting her teeth. I called her a tough Minnesota Indian, and she said, "I hope I'm one, and keep the show going while I'm here, will you?"

We did our best, and it worked quite well when Papa had us out for dinner with him Sunday evening. The gloom button was hit but once. "It's hell, rattling around in this big strange house all by yourself." Till took it fast.

"Yes, Papa, I know all about it; don't we old farmers say that we take the water for granted until the well goes dry?"

He gave her a frowning stare that slowly softened. Yes, he guessed that was the way of it; he was pretty demanding of his well, too, and, "Don't say that you know it because I know you do, Miss Till."

They let Mary come home on Monday, and rare as it was for me to lead off, I did that time: suggested to Papa we take a run down to Silver Creek. He readily agreed, and we had a fair take on a couple of bends on the main stream, handy to the road. Ours was not a very talkative two hours or so, and since Tillie and I were leaving the next day around noon, the happy thought came to me that in our freezer was something to lift his spirits, a little anyway: he'd gone for quite a while without some good fresh fish — I had them. While working in east Idaho at the end of the season, I took a weekend day to fish Palisades Reservoir on the upper Snake River with friends — who saw that I had "plenty" over my own catch. They were no less than dream fish; cutthroat trout averaging a half-yard long, quick-frozen with all of their fresh good in them. I rolled newspapers around four of the biggest ones, and Till phoned that I was on my way. If I had taken a few gold ingots I doubt they'd have made half the hit. He bounded up into the kitchen as I walked in the opposite door: "Hi, Mr. Pappy. Hey, watcha got, kid?" In rapid-fire, for that long package did not look usual with me, nor was I ever associated with fish. Papers flew as leaves before a wind. Hearing the commotion, Mary came, wincing at every jarring step.

"Kitner, at one sitting can you work your way around one beauty trout as long as from your good elbow to your fingertips?"

"Well! . . . I'll bet I can get up one side of one, anyway."

"Hmph! There'll be no cotsy scraps from these, old Pelican Papa will see to that . . . tails, heads and gill plates look good enough to eat . . . you couldn't have timed them better, kid, but you're not . . ."

"No, not emptying the box just for a few days, Papa, we have more."

The old file box dished up the fact that the first fish feed we ever sat down to were cutthroats, "but not ball bats like these." He came out to the car with "the stranger dressed up in city clothes" to send his best regards to the man he'd never met, Vince Hunter, but had heard many fine things about, and to whom he owed a drink, if I ever managed to get him up to Idaho at the right time.

"I will, Papa. See you Saturday, for sure. Old man Hunter is going on vacation, so I know we won't get stuck."

We were not — bumped into Mary and Papa at the market, saw his Buick station wagon there when we drove into town. Nothing would do but that we come out to the house when finished with our shopping — the boys were coming to shoot a round of targets. But one real purpose was

to know that there was no change in my working plans. Second, to let us know, since attention to Mary's arm required it, they would be in Idaho for some time — meaning Christmas. The subject opened after we'd shot, over a short one in the kitchen, Papa only lukewarm at first. As the pace increased, so did his, and shortly he was leading it, going all-out over Mary's ebullience. She had a good cook in Lola — even he could roast the turkey, if necessary — Duke was assigned to "traditionally run down another goose," and since they now had a roof of their own over them, it was only right that Christmas dinner be at the house of Hemingway! Any arguments?

How the hell do you go against an order of the general — General? That's what the general thought all along! And as I would be working at Idaho Falls right up near to Christmas, would I be so good as to bear the invitation to Dort and old pilot Hill to join the fun? Yes, indeed, I would do that, but wondered how I'd squeeze in time to sneak out for the Christmas trees. Oh, just bring your thirst and a hunger as your contribution, but if you run into a real delicacy, it'll be as welcome as you.

Which is just about the way it was for the preliminary, for truth is, the buildup was cover-up of keen disappointment that Christmas could not be at their own home in Cuba. Though there was no open talk of it, the evidence was very obvious — and why not? My point is that, shaken, troubled as he was, I can only credit the outward show of exuberant anticipation to a discipline beyond the likes of me. In another way of putting it: there would be a best-substitute Christmas — somewhere — come hell and high snowbanks.

He worried about me driving the tricky road, in a questionable-weather time of year, through the Craters of the Moon lava to and from Idaho Falls — for the four trips I'd have: "Take that hell's-frozen-over son of a bitch easy now, kid, won't you?"

Christmas in Ketchum, Idaho.

He was right, and didn't need to tell me (it had become second nature to me by then), so I made it a point to call home by company line when I arrived. A laughable parallel of the past and present came up in my first week there. I was out to the Hill house one evening, wishing that I had been with Pete that morning. Normally not good so late in season, luck smiled on him — a pair of small Canada geese. Papa had asked "no presents," stressing it a bit, and none amounting to anything was planned at all. Naturally, Pete's geese would grace the table, his contribution; Till would roast them, knocking out the need of "His Highness the Duke's" domestic bird. I put in a phone call, got Mary, heard the chatter in the kitchen — Papa and Duke just in from hunting, Tillie there, the lineup just right. Pete talked to Mary in thanks, then asked for the man of the house.

"This is the old coyote speaking, what service might he render you, Mr. Pete?"

Mr. P. wished to know about all the old guff of no presents. Well, if it was a brand that he hadn't tried — but he thought he knew them all. Oh, yes, he knew the brand well enough, and they'd come high, but not quite high enough — right over the pit that morning. There was complete silence for all of about three seconds, then: Over the "pit" — had he heard it? Yes, about forty yards over it — withdraw now?

"Why, hell yes, I withdraw it, they sound like Canucks to me, Pete, and say, the old dog's on scent of a turkey, saw him a day or two ago — tied to a leg of the butcher's block!"

One thing spurs another, so a gag present for "the pot" in order that Duke and I could hold up tradition: I'd heard of a butcher in Jackson, Wyoming, who made heavenly salami, his base, pure wild elk meat — common as dudes in summer in that area — so Pete saw that we got a "wagon-tongue" of it — meaning, for true, that it was put up in "gut" as big around as a man's fist and as long as his arm — out-of-this-world stuff, and a bite of it sent your senses somewhere else. That package took a back seat for nothing, went well into the new year — in several places. But, as to the pre-Christmas:

My working places shut down, I drove home on December 23, in bright weather, the road good. By noon of the twenty-fourth snow was coming down with a vengeance, and in a short while Papa rapped on our window with his alpenstock — snow water dripping off his whiskers, the mood good, but worrying about how it might be howling down out there in "Mr. Dante's country" that the Hills would have to drive across. He'd walked into town, to the market, and thought he'd better come up and we'd call Arco — midway to Idaho Falls.

"I've already talked to Pete, Papa. It's coming down out there, all right — if a single flake of snow looks about for a place to fall in Idaho, that's the place it picks, as you damn well know. But it's young yet, they're on their way."

Then, purely on impulse, I laughed outright, said that if we merely touched on a subject, damned if it didn't happen, even though I had beaten the weather and the lousy road. He gave me the one-sided owlish grin.

"You mean ol' Papa's spooks are rubbing off on you after listening to them so long?"

In rarity for such stops on his frequent walks, he doffed his parka to talk a while; the picture on Mary's arm was brighter by then, though plenty of attention was given it in whirlpool and other treatments made possible by a split, removable cast. He merely mentioned it, preferring to talk the subject at hand: Mary's pretty tree, her old-fashioned touch in lighting it with genuine tallow candles; and if Sir Till, who had never roasted a wild goose in her life, would stuff them with apple as the old-timers used to do. When he got up to go, you couldn't see two blocks toward town center, but: "It's warm, not under thirty, walking in a good snow is the best there is . . . but check in with us when the kids get in, will you?"

They made it at a crawling pace, the storm still at it. Mary and Papa went to the Saviers' house on Christmas Eve, the little sister of their three young boys thinking Santa came early that year and didn't have much to do! The Hills and we went out for dinner, at the new Christiania Restaurant a mere three blocks from the house on the Sun Valley road. Afterward, the sky was star-studded, the streets not plowed in our neighborhood; we got stuck coming up the hill — a low-bellied car entirely at fault? — then sat around a good half the night listening to good music that the *same* Santa had a hand in 365 days before.

The weatherman stayed friendly, we shot some clay targets in midafternoon when Duke got off shift; and if your score was a dozen or more broken of a stack of fifteen you got a tongue-wetting nip from the bottle of Tavel sitting in a hole in the snow under the rail bordering the drive. Our dinner party was small: three couples of us, bachelor Duke, and Lola — far from home in a snowy white world sharply contrasting with her own. Mary's lovely table was set for eight.

I took a Rolleiflex out with me, flashbulbs for one roll of film; the truly fine time recorded by it is better than any words of mine.

9.

A Stormy Season

By prearrangement I worked the first half of January right at home, and in nearby high-country snowfields, filming water sources for my irrigation documentary. By an odd quirk it was both ideal subject matter and the most miserable period of weather I could remember in my mountain experience — above-normal snowfall with emphasis on cold. I also had quite a bit of idle time for these very reasons, a trying period. I did experience one unheard-of thing: I had rough "work prints" of both my major films on hand, sent up by our studio for reviewing purposes, and on one stormy day Papa Hemingway sat with me for an hour in our dining room "theater" looking at subject matter that I figured would bore him silly. Well, he stayed on, saying, "You get around an awful lot of country, and now I know how to irrigate and grow potatoes."

In sharp contrast, I drove down out of the Boulder Mountains one "dry blizzard" day so cold that when I pulled up behind Papa walking back toward town on the highway and opened the door for him, he hopped right in with no questions — except what in hell was either of us doing out on such a day? When you saw him wearing gloves while out for a walk you knew it was cold. He had brought his car into town for some minor thing, got a little exercise while waiting for it — half of it sitting by our fire after I picked him up. Need I say that such conditions brought on that restless, what-do-I-do-next disease called shack-happy? There was no covering up and denying it; he wasn't writing worth a goddamn, nothing sounded right when he got it down. He again opened up the subject of incorporating, one he'd made quite a to-do of the winter before; would we come in with our names? Sure we will, Papa, just as before, to satisfy the requirement of corporate law. Oh, hell, he wouldn't go for that — no "dollar-a-year name" in an outfit of his, just as he'd said — the taxes saved would do everybody some good. Well, he got off that one some way, maybe in his acceptance of a bite of salami and a small glass of wine — just looking at the blowing snow outside would suggest that. It went from one thing to another so fast that you wondered which to answer.

One blessing in that interim was the trapshooting; somehow, a session was managed nearly every day — for one special reason besides the obvious one. Doc Saviers would stop on his way home to lunch, check in with Mary, check Papa's blood pressure — and not upon George's insistence, by a long way. It got to be a sort of daily routine, when we were available — out came the guns, a case of targets, then everything was great, and you loved it. The kick the gals got out of our antics, watching from Mary's big upstairs window, was as good a spur as our own competitive efforts — and they were just that, no mistake.

One afternoon around four o'clock we saw Mary and Papa at the market, she doing the shopping, pushing her cart with one hand, Papa just standing by himself up front near the door — dejected, morose, way off somewhere. At whatever our greeting was, he said, oh, he wasn't up to much of anything, he was just the chauffeur, the errand boy around his establishment. In my clumsy way I said, weren't we all erranders in one way or another as we went along. Yeah, but I was an adaptable boy, he was just an old dog incapable of learning new tricks. He grinned as his sentence died, said, "Come on, Mr. Pappy, we're no good here. Let's go across the street . . . join us, Miss Till, when you and Miss Mary finish, huh?"

Across the street was the Christiania Restaurant's bar, a bar that Papa liked before the after-ski hour crowded it too much. It was the sort of weather to start such an hour a little early, but it wasn't bad yet and we sat alone at the end of the bar, talking to an old skiing friend of mine to whom I introduced Papa. They were hitting it off good, an empty stool between them — and that was too bad. A stranger strode up, paid no attention to any of us, and sat down on it, loudly called for a drink for himself. A blind man could tell that he did not know who he sat beside, but a deaf man could hear him — any talk was his talk. Well, we were just about to get out of there when our gals came in, stopping at a table of some locals. At that precise moment the loud man turned and asked Papa if he had high-altitude, dry-air skin trouble, or did he wear the beard for effect?

Good God, sailors, I thought, clear the decks! My back was to the wall — the end stool — and a whole mountain of suede leather vest, Papa's back, rose up in front of me. I shook in my ski boots as he put his parka down on the bar, his old stocking cap on it. But he controlled himself, got the man told off in no uncertain terms — a very soft, deadly voice — then turned to tell me he'd go out to order drinks for the girls. He hoped it would be more pleasant when he came back. Surprisingly, his expression was quite calm, a cold glitter in his eye. The beard was a touchy subject, especially in the ski-crowded community where, likely as not, you could see a purple beard on an elephant. The man paid no attention to me, nor to my friend, while we tried to exchange a little talk in which he asked how long I'd known Mr. Hemingway — a long time, as he recalled — and he addressed me as Pappy. The loud-mouth spoke up, said, "So that's who he is, and you use a form of his name, huh?"

He was big enough to chew me up and spit me out, but I saw so much red in the atmosphere as I came off my stool that I didn't see Papa appear behind our charming company as it got up from its perch. It felt a forefinger jab hard on its shoulder, a cold

voice saying, "Listen, my friend pirates nothing from nobody — it was his name long before I knew him, which is a hell of a long time — but you pirated this little privacy of ours at the end of this bar . . . come on, Mr. Pappy, it's not a good end anymore."

He apologized to my friend. We worked

Though Cuba had its charms, this was Papa's country.

our way to the open entrance to the room to wait for the girls. I'll give the intruder credit, though: while I held Papa's parka for him, the man caught my eye, plainly signaling that he'd come to apologize. I shook my head because I feared for him. Needlessly, perhaps, but — I'd seen the temper before.

Papa said in a moment, "Jesus, kid, I've never seen you so hot. You had me scared."

"So was I scared, Papa," and he replied with a disgusted half-grin, "The son of a bitch. . . . What was it your dad said . . . funny how there's so many more in the world than horses to go with 'em?" That was the end of it — for a while.

The intent was to come back to the Christiania for dinner; Papa had mentioned it when we left the market, said he felt the need, and he knew Mary did — her frequent, nerve-wracking treatments were worse than the discomfiture of a healing break itself. She'd come from one that afternoon, so instead of going out, we had a simple pickup evening meal at their house. I went up to Papa's room to help him flatten a bit too much tilt in his writing stand. He was talkative, as we did a temporary job with no tools, openly said he'd be so glad when the doctors released Miss Mary so they could get back to the Finca where he always wrote well. And there were people to do the menial jobs he was saddled with now.

"But we hate to leave, Mr. Pappy, truly we do . . . can you remember a time when I didn't hate to leave this country?"

Tired from her treatment, Mary went up to bed early, Till with her to help "unbutton me." There was half a bottle of wine left, the fire burning low. I was asked to toss another log on it — only ten o'clock.

When I sat down at the table again, Papa's clenched fist was grinding the palm of his other hand, and he was saying to himself more than to me, "So, he wanted to know if I wear the beard for effect, the son of a. . . ."

"Aw, Papa . . . that was more booze talking than sense. Probably had a bad skiing day. . . ."

He glared a hole in me while I plowed right on that the man had wanted to apologize, but that I had headed him off because I was in the mood to take him on myself, once safely out, my back away from a wall. I got a feeble grin for the quick footwork, but it faded on sight of Tillie coming back. She knew nothing of the incident, got a full account of it; so obviously the long simmering had greased the skids, skid being a mild term for what flowed forth: Everything was going wrong, against his efforts at work; the doctors he knew were dragging their feet; Mary was dragging hers, it was all costing a fortune; she wanted to wait until her cast was off, which he knew would be a long time; he could go by himself, but he'd not leave her behind — hell, anything could develop when a man deserts his wife when she's in trouble. Why, a gal just might tell a man to go to hell for that sort of thing.

I was about to try a tack, but the signs said no, it was woman's work, keep out. Had I done so, my head might be in orbit yet. Tillie waited for an opening, very patiently, and when she got it she held on stubbornly, simply telling him that he was being most unfair in belaboring a scapegoat. Scapegoat? — that was a mighty rough term for Miss Till to be using. Yes, indeed, and so was his attitude a rough one. Accidents happened to everyone, he put a slant of deliberateness on it; wasn't it worth some mutual patience toward his Miss Mary having a good and usable arm instead of a stiff one? And just where did he get such ideas of the situation developing into anything as drastic as he hinted?

December 25, 1959. Christmas in Ketchum, Idaho at Hemingway's house.

"Nothing is further from the truth, Papa, I know it and so do you."

She had no choice but to be her honest and loyal self — or risk being labeled a phony in appeasing him. He didn't slow up easily, but slow up he did, eventually, and thanked her for her fairness. And, God's miracle, she got a little chuckle from him when he remembered once asking her if she truly thought he was no angel to live with. She said yes, in exactly the way he expected her to. When we left he went outside with us for a check on the weather — "cold enough to make a coyote howl off key."

But the evening shook us to our foundations, nonetheless: we were not total strangers to occasional evidence of hallucinatory amblings, small inventions on this and that; nor of magnifications, overly-severe criticism. Well, you say to yourself, it can't be too long until a letup of tension is due, and it wasn't long.

On Monday, January 11, her arm in a removable cast, the doctors released Mary. At once train reservations were applied for, came through for Sunday, the seventeenth, meaning a late Saturday night departure to catch the Union Pacific's crack "City of Portland" at the beastly hour of 2:00 A.M. in Shoshone. Preparations commenced immediately, spirits high; the show was about to get on the road again.

In July of 1960 a letter arrived from Mary:

Papa is fine, has worked prodigiously on his bullfight thing from last summer, which Life *will publish and then will go into a book by Scribners.*

Now we're getting ready for a vacation from here — Papa going to Spain to collect the final dope for his book, a comparatively

146

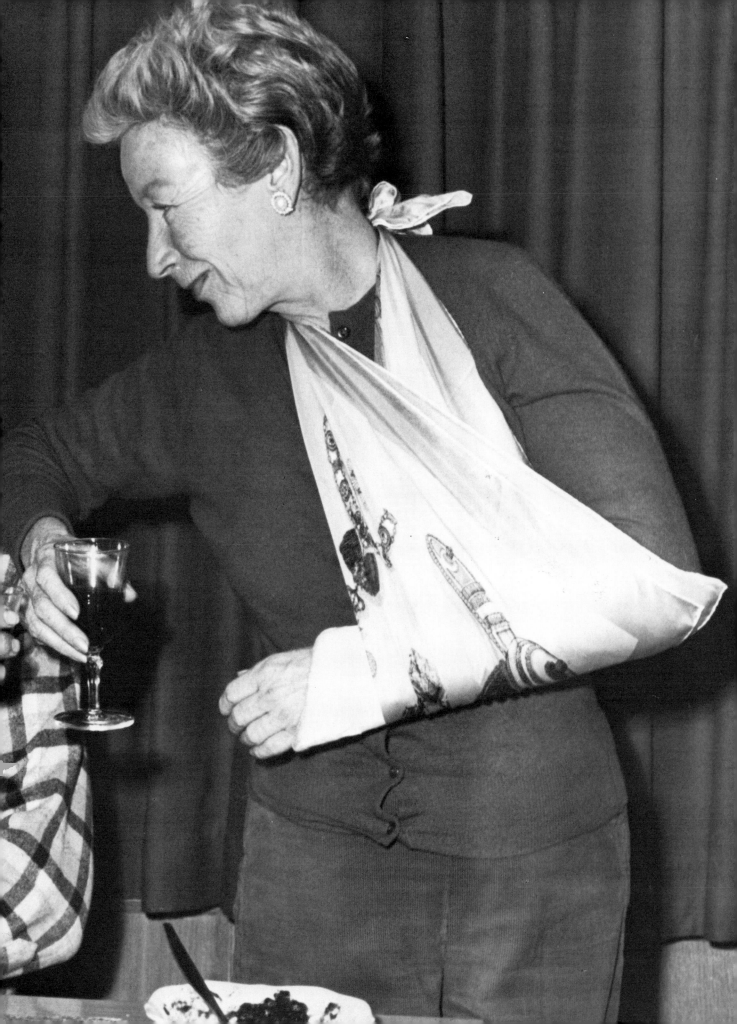

short journey he now thinks, about six weeks. I will go up to New York and spend the time more or less fixing up our apartment there. Then going out to Ketchum, either with a detour to here, or straight from New York.

Thinking about this, it occurred to me that Miss Till has never seen New York, she might like to, and with our apartment more or less liveable it would cost neither you nor us anything more than the train fare if she'd like to come.

She went on to say they planned to leave Cuba between the twenty-sixth and thirtieth of July, and asked Till's reply before then, or awaiting them in New York. Till wrote to the latter address, advising that we had problems and: "Will come if at all possible." The deterrent was an extremely dry summer, heavy demands on water; we had a big yard of grass and flowers, and Tillie was handling all "the farming," which she could not find anyone to do for her. She was still on the fence when on August 16, Mary wrote from New York, her letter opening with this:

They had a lot of nonsense on the radio last Monday — August 8, about Papa being very ill in Spain — it took me 9 hours to find out the truth, every minute agony — all false.

Papa got off for Spain (by air) on August 4, to finish up all the dirty little chores that he has to do before he can finish either the Life *piece or his book. . . .*

It was something of a sweat getting away from Cuba, and we don't know what will happen to our stuff there, our whole both lives' treasures, actually. I'll tell you about it when I see you. There's nothing we can do about it at the moment.

I intended to go back to Cuba for a week or two in September, but now they make the entering and leaving so complicated that I think I'll stay here — waiting to hear from Papa.

She did not return to Cuba, which we learned in her reply to Tillie's word that going east was impossible for some time. Conjecture on our part, yes, but it was quite obvious from the limited news of the day that their Finca might as well be written off. Sensing that Papa himself had left it for the last time, Till said of herself, "I should say to hell with my yard full of work and at least go and help Mary cry — in our own way."

10.

The Short, Dark Fall of '60

That fall the Hemingways arrived by train. Doc Saviers met the "City of Portland" in Shoshone and we were waiting at their house when they arrived at ten that night. I should liken it to a reunion, for the ten long months had seemed like so many years — and it was a soul-warming year, too. While doing some winter preparation jobs, I got careless with a power saw and almost lost a joint or two of my right forefinger — my "shootin' finger." The doctor saved it for me, but immobilized it in a metal stall which ruled out any late season duck shooting.

Mary's arm was good for hugging — and shooting; Papa's, like those on an octopus. As ebullient as ever, the faint traces of travel weariness were hardly noticed. When presence of mind finally got us inside the house he took hold of my hand like it was an object of reverence, likened its metallic protuberance to a 20mm antiaircraft shell, wanted to know how I worked with it.

"Don't have too much of that kind to do, Papa, but I'm a fair bird dog."

He was full of questions of things local, of our plans, asking of them right down to dates — all satisfactory. An amusing exchange was his in-person thanks for a letter I'd written back in the spring and of which Mary had written about later. In it I'd sent a picture of those hordes of wintering ducks on Snake River. Neatly encased in his comments on the nearly unbelievable photograph was his apology for that cold night on the road. I said, "Maybe come December I'll have enough of this iron off so that I can trigger a gun."

"The old doctor says you might, but he doubts it. How about it, George?"

"If he wants to keep it all, he damn well better mind Scott Earle," George said.

"Sure, kid, I've never backed you up in my whole life, but for a modest fee, ol' Papa can keep us in birds, won't we, citizens?"

In the few days I was home, we knew it was going to be good: Papa got his fingers into the organizing; was pleased to get the familiar old rented Chevy he'd once had; got into the marketing up to his chin, and a very first renewal of the old was a picnic, hardly ahead of fully stocking the pantry. Pheasant season was not yet open, it was overly warm for ducks, and for a change, perhaps inspired over the view from his "working window," he steered it north by the river at the foot of the Boulder Range. The dry season made for a "beauty fall" of color, some departing, but the aspen still a flaming gold, sumac the deep hue of pigeon's blood, the willows rimming the river a shimmering, coppery green in the mountain breeze.

It was good to see Papa take the wheel because he wanted to; for once he was not catching hell for freezing his back-seat passengers with a rolled-down window; hearing him say, "Let's go on over Galena Summit to the lookout place, just to feast our eyes on the Salmon River headwaters country, the Sawtooth Valley, the one to end all mountain valleys . . . anywhere that I have seen, anyway . . . we haven't been over for two years, Kitner, when we brought the Bruces, remember?"

While taking in the magnificent vista that can stir you to the depths, I mentioned that I had some scouting to do, when the big cattle herds moved out of the summer range in the lower valley and Stanley Basin to the winter range downriver around Challis; hinted that a trip or two with me be considered. Papa said, "Great, we'll put in our order that this weather stays so good." In late spring, when the wild flowers turned much of the valley and the lower basin into an unbelievable carpet of color, it was definitely planned that I make the opening of my new subject there — which I also mentioned only as a matter of course. Papa said, "We've heard so much about it, and in all the years, we've never seen it in summer. I wonder why. Well, we will." Then with the I-told-you-so look, he offered to bet that I would propose to use what we could of Bud Purdy's fine cattle operation at Silver Creek. I said that I certainly did

intend to, and he replied, "It figures, Bud is so damn loyal to friends . . . how would we have gotten along so well for so long without him?"

Back on Wood River at a little Forest Service place, we singed our fingers on the baked beans can, ate ash-sprinkled,

fire-charred hot dogs skewered on green willow sticks; we had small beers chilled in the fringe-iced river, Papa tippled from a small bottle of red. He wouldn't let me help put out our fire but he hauled enough glass-thin sheets of ice from the stream "to put out the Chicago fire . . . we burn up no

A small herd of elk on the lower slopes of Adams Butte.

Hunting on the Purdy Ranch outside of Ketchum, Idaho.

country with our litter-bugging."

It was in the winter of 1960 that Papa's behavior began to change more and more. He often looked dejected and morose. He complained about the old gang breaking up; not exactly harping on it, but still you knew it bothered him. Mary persuaded him at this time to undergo a full checkup at the Mayo Clinic. They left soon after.

Not fancying ourselves as even amateur analysts of the situation, we tried to creep inside Papa's head — came up with the logic that Mayo's was mainly thought of as for the *physically* sick; so wouldn't the difficulty be cloaked in something like hypertension? Which is what we soon learned as correct analysis. Surely, his own actions led us to be certain that Papa knew something had to be done.

In answer to my immediate letter, Mary called us not so long afterward, her first word that they would not be back by Christmas. Was it all right to write directly to Papa? By all means, please do, she said, and did we have any morsels at the moment — she was on her way to see him then — something they could share? I hesitated to say that I had been hunting a couple of times, and had done well, fairly normal again. She would not sort that out, she said, Papa would be delighted. An item in my schedule, that she knew of, had matured: I was to be home much of the winter, making a ski technique film for Sun Valley promotion, and a short specialty subject for television use. It was lucky, a "tuck-in" that I could do in the otherwise slow time in my regular program. So Mary said, "Great," and went on to say, "Shoot us a duck or two, and eat them for us, because I can't tell you more now, except that I have

hopes of us getting out of here sometime in January." When she wrote later that they were having Christmas dinner at the home of one of Papa's doctors, well — that more than matched the simple Christmas that we had with the Hills. Like a small boy, I had the warmness of knowing that in our own "cool, well-ventilated place" there were ducks curing and some put away. Mary was correspondent, and the news was increasingly good, but by mid-January there still was nothing definite as to their return.

Papa and Mary did return late that winter. There were some reunions, some dinners, and some warmhearted laughter. But Papa did not look or act like his old self.

As planned, I worked close to home that spring, so we saw Papa often and it was not good, not at all. Then on Saturday, April 22, we felt the cold fingers of premonition. To me, at least, it was reminiscent of our little circle gripping the arms of our seats in the darkened theater of doom, before an ugly curtain that could open anytime — and, of course, we were just that. You feel like crawling under anything at hand when trying to make talk, get nowhere, no matter what you say — thinking: My God, is this Papa, like a deaf man who sees the fun going on before him, joins in with a grin like on a mask? Then the fleeting moments of his efforts to make it good — like it once was. I'm sure that for myself, I recall it as the first time that I truly wanted to run — from a game that you can't win for losing; nor could I even wishfully think that anyone would win this one, unless something was done, and done fast. It was — on Sunday.

On his usual call at the house that forenoon, Doc Saviers saw at one glance that it was time to act. He did, and without resistance of any kind got Papa to the Sun Valley hospital. Long later in the day we learned that arrangements were all set to fly Papa back to the Mayo Clinic in Rochester — Larry Johnson would be waiting at Hailey with his plane ready at eight o'clock Monday morning. Fully informed of the day's happenings, I shuddered in wondering if Papa would resist a return to what he surely must have known would be a nightmare to him. I resisted the thought that he would — but it was a persistent one, and it was still around when I left town the following morning and saw Larry warming up his plane as I drove past the Hailey airstrip about a quarter to eight.

I was on a short job that trip and returned around noon on Wednesday, and again I saw Larry on his hangar ramp. I could not go on without stopping to ask him how their trip had been. He said, fine, except that he'd had minor engine trouble that was fixed at their one stop for fuel; then he added that they'd been home but a short while, the trip had been delayed until Tuesday morning. I knew that Mary was not slated to go that time, but I asked Larry no more and went on, wondering why the delay. I got it — voluntarily — from a friend who was asked at the last minute on Monday morning to go along. Thoughtfully, he stopped at our house that evening when he saw my road car out front.

It would be gracious not to put down the true facts of that crucial time; but I do because they've been publicly reported in distorted, magnified, and, in part, purely fabricated form. In short, dramatized, from information gained at a distance, so to speak, and not from eyewitnesses and participants. Such reporting is unjust, unfair to Papa Hemingway — and God knows it's difficult enough to write the truth of an old friend on that sort of rough road. So, to set the record straight:

At the hospital that Monday morning, April 24, Doc Saviers and Papa were about to take off for Hailey; then George happened upon Don Anderson passing by, and with good reason asked him to make the trip. Taken by surprise, and not at all prepared for it, Don saw the reason and agreed to go — time the factor, about a seven-hour flight to Rochester in normal conditions.

George needed a few more minutes for other matters before leaving, so he asked Don to take his own car and drive Papa out home for some personal things that he refused to go without; George would follow within minutes in his car for their drive to Hailey, where he'd leave it. Nurse Joan Higgons went along to bring back Don's car.

Out at the house — at the back door — Don got out when Papa did, who said Don needn't come in, his things were upstairs where Mary was, he'd be down in minutes. Don was at his heels anyway, so close they practically went in as one; then Don was alone, for Papa took off like a shot. Don beckoned to Joan and followed him; at the corner gun rack in the living room, from behind him, Don pinned Papa's arms as he closed the breech on his double-barrel shotgun, and managed to get a thumb on the gun's opening lever. Joan pulled out the shells and the brief storm subsided immediately. The struggle was brisk but short, neither man off his feet or hurt in any way. George was there about as it ended, and Papa went quietly to the hospital again, for that day — the flight reset for a daylight takeoff Tuesday morning. That one went off on schedule, with no resistance of any kind evident — except a single question: "Where are they taking me this time?"

Having flown the trip before, Larry's flight plan was simplicity itself, aided by geographical oddity. Lay a ruler on a map and see that it is a beeline from Hailey to Rochester, Minnesota, with Rapid City, South Dakota, almost exactly halfway of the distance and squarely on the ruler's edge. A busy airline stop, a port with facilities, this was the planned stop for fuel. Larry used his single-engine four-place Piper Apache airplane. The weather was good, with a brisk tail wind as an advantage. Ahead out of Idaho the high Tetons had to be climbed over, the plane heavily loaded, its cabin cramped. George rode "co-pilot" up front with Larry, Papa and Don in the rear seats — Don a smaller man, but husky, tipped the scales at about Papa's current weight. About an hour out, the old leather belt that Papa had clung to for more years than I can recall parted under its buckle, and Papa quietly asked if they might go back so he could get another. George turned to say it would be rough bucking the head wind over the Tetons, so Don appeased the situation by pulling off his own belt, and Papa accepted it — managed somehow in the tight confines to replace his old one with it.

The good pushing wind was luck, for farther along over Wyoming, Larry had to nurse his engine, but still managed the landing at Rapid City in good time. There it was discovered that a coil on one magneto was burned out, so the refueling stop for both passengers and plane stretched to something over an hour. Repairs were about finished when a twin-engine Aero, Commander landed and taxied to a parking place on the transient aircraft apron where Larry's plane was parked nearby. As many of us might do, Papa stood at a wingtip of the Piper, appearing fascinated with the spinning props as the pilot revved the Commander's engines in, clearing them for the cutoff. Both George and Don noticed it, and so Don moved over to say they were about ready to go. They were; the engine satisfied Larry, and the balance of the trip was smooth and easy.

At Rochester, Papa greeted his doctors warmly, even jocularly; George phoned Mary back in Ketchum that all was well, and the Piper got the men as far toward home as Rapid City, where they spent the night, completing the second leg the next morning.

So, it was natural that Larry told me their trip was fine, and passed off lightly their delay for minor repairs at Rapid City — there was nothing else for him to say. If there had been anything unusual, Larry would have told me — quietly. That weekend I ran into George Saviers, and talked a couple of minutes with him. I invaded his realm only to say that I couldn't

envy his role as both doctor and friend; his reply was a shake of his head in man-to-man feeling.

Not long afterward, in one of my routine calls to California, I asked for the going word on Coop, who had been seriously ill for quite some time. It was going, all right, in respectful whispers; the window was closed, so I was told, the finale not far off. My informant was right.

I was driving home, across a stretch of open lonely country, on Saturday, May 13, my car radio turned on, something I very seldom did in driving alone. Paying little attention to its low drone, I was suddenly alerted, realized that I'd heard Gary Cooper's name, that I was listening to a Los Angeles newscast. Coop had died quietly in sleep early that morning, at his home in Holmby Hills. I expected it, yes, but shock came, nonetheless, and like in dreams, countless hours and as many miles in Coop's company down the long years went by me in seconds. I said aloud, "Good-bye, Coop, it's been fun, all of it."

Indeed, it had, and still a couple of hours from home, I wondered for most of it how that news might have been received elsewhere. As to that, I never heard.

From latter May on, following Mary's departure for Rochester, we had infrequent news from there — mainly good. The best news from that second sojourn came from Papa himself — in the form of a letter. He wrote it to the second of the Saviers boys, a lad not yet in his teens, plagued with a chronic illness. It was a masterpiece in Papa's own handwriting, and so typically him, so touchingly appealing, that eventually it was reproduced in full in a summer issue of *Life* magazine.

There had been, however, some words a time or two that were not exactly encouraging. From mid-June on was a blank — and understandable, as we later learned. It was at month's end, a Friday

Correspondents Mary and Papa Hemingway re-sponding to a season's worth of letters.

evening, June 30, that I came home and we went to a big noisy cocktail party where we heard in an aside almost at once that the Hemingways had arrived unannounced but a short while before. Surprised no end, a first thought was to sneak back home to our telephone; but of course it was too soon for that, and there was a bonus with the good news, too. A Hertz car was rented back in Minnesota, and to do the driving to Idaho, Papa's old friend, retired gymnasium operator George Brown, had come out from New York. We considered that a good sign — for over many years we had heard such fine things about George, the genius in a boxing ring of whom Papa always said he was never allowed to so much as touch his perfect nose with a glove, let alone hurt it; so naturally it was good to know that he'd called on this respected friend.

At the time I was just starting to work close to home, coming in each night from the Salmon River country, the Sawtooth Valley, and down farther around Stanley Basin. It was a good "water" year and never had I seen the country as verdantly beautiful. On Saturday morning I had a short job to do over there, and of course I recalled us talking about this very same country the fall before — when Papa wished that he'd known it in summer. Now I was sure that he would — and I would nudge that a bit with a natural: propose an outing over there for the weekend. My enthusiasm was dampened somewhat when I returned home for a late lunch. Tillie was almost in tears.

Shortly before, she had pulled in at the market, saw a strange car pull in a few spaces from hers, and saw that its passenger was Papa. Fine, she thought, just right, happening upon him like this. She was just opening her door to greet him when he went hurrying into the store — a dozen feet from her car — looking neither left nor right, tensed in manner, and so shockingly thin and gaunt that to her he appeared several inches taller. Her voice was shaky

when she told me, "I was a coward, I know, but if I had gone in that store and come face to face with Papa, I'm sure I'd have burst out in tears, and wouldn't that have been a fine thing to do?"

She backed out and drove up home, went back a bit later, when she had a few minutes with Chuck (he was a bit disturbed also, Papa had been so jittery in the few words he had with him), then went back farther in the store when George Brown came in. Chuck asked him about their trip out, and George said it was fine, until they got into old familiar country well out in Wyoming, then it couldn't go fast enough — checking progress by the road map and watch, concern for tires, impatience over stops for gas, and the like. But there was a good note in George's chat with Chuck: he and Papa had been to the lumberyard that morning, had a heavy panel of plywood cut for rigging up a table to be out on the sunny south terrace at Papa's house; George was to stay on a while, and use his physiotherapy skill on his old friend. Hearing that, well, it was the best word yet. I had some month's-end paperwork, some phoning to do that afternoon, and I threatened several times to interrupt it, so we could drive out to say hello. I didn't interrupt myself, for in all of this — especially Tillie's one look at Papa — a thought kept nagging at me: If Papa was like this, why was he home? Had he talked himself out of the place back there? I had a suspicion that it was something like that, and in spite of all the factors, I know that I never once underestimated the "force" that was Papa himself. Those ebbs and flows I remembered too well. Later, I got more than a mild hint in confirmation of my suspicion.

Be that as it may, we didn't go out to the house, or call — we thought it best to wait; then in good time, Sunday forenoon, we'd call Mary and suggest taking a drive over the summit, maybe take along a picnic basket. That idea at least had merit, the weather was absolutely perfect. We were dated for the evening with old friends from out of town, and our foursome ended up at the Christiania Bar not far from midnight, for a nightcap on our way home. There we learned that Mary, Papa, and George Brown had been there for a quietly pleasant dinner. Papa, quite jovial, had had a fine wine with his meal, had even chided a waitress when she poured him a refill from a near empty bottle, allowing a bit of the dregs to reach his glass. They had left for home but a short while before we dropped in.

When we turned off our light that night the overall scene was brighter. Alas, it was but a flash of brightness.

Epilogue

In those last tense weeks when Papa was away, I so often thought of his remark: "The truly good and wonderful things you can know but once in a life."

He tried for quite a long time to know as many more as he could, and settled for picking up some pieces of the old ones. He frankly told me that at the end of the last truly good fall he knew here in Idaho — the 1958 fall. It was the night I found him sitting on the floor in our sitting room — when the mood was good, if a bit pensive.

No one will ever know — nor does it matter, really — when Papa decided that it wasn't any good. The awesome twin blast of his favorite shotgun was his announcement that it was not. It was Sunday morning, July 2, 1961 — nineteen days short of his sixty-second year. Some reporter wrote that it was a shot heard round the world. An old

phrase, but how true. I needn't dwell on that time — it's Hemingway history, some theory — but I have a thought or two about it that I want to leave for what they are worth; they are strictly my own, and from a man's point of view.

Papa's dilemma was many-sided, but I do know that paramount was a deep humiliation. Observation tells me that he fought with all he had against doing what he did — he was against it, and wrote so in his own works, albeit as fiction. I did not know Papa as a man without God, so I'm sure that he did not *want* to kill himself. I pass on these views, not in biased defense of him, but because I feel it his due. He did care what would be thought about it, as he cared all his life what he was thought of. I figure that he was certain he wasn't his own man anymore and he was not about to face the *living* death. I did not live behind those

160

lovable brown eyes, eyes that saw the view in true perspective, I'm quite sure. If it wasn't some courage at work that fateful Sunday morning, then I don't know what else it was.

We buried Papa Hemingway in the rather quaint but pretty little cemetery here in Ketchum on July 6. As a pallbearer with mutual local friends, I felt again that strange indescribable loneliness that I'd known twice before in the same small area — the first time twenty-two years back, when we were both pallbearers, and a beautiful tribute was read; then twenty years later when we buried the colonel beside Gene Van Guilder. Yes, I was lonely, but I cannot truly say that I mourned. "That was the way of the Plan, and we can't tamper with it." Destiny does indeed write some strange scripts.

Five summers later a simple close-to-nature memorial to Papa was dedicated in public ceremony a short way out of Ketchum overlooking Trail Creek.

Someone said, "A memorial to Ernest Hemingway? Who ever left more of a memorial than he did to himself — his legacy to us all?" He was looking at the ample bronze base plaque on the simple rocky footing supporting a pedestaled sculptured Hemingway head, and he added in a soft voice, "But he unknowingly contributed a bit to this one."

The words on the plaque are excerpts from the Gene Van Guilder eulogy, chosen by writers, then edited to finality by one of them — Miss Mary. Who, I wonder, would approve of them more than the man who wrote them?

> BEST OF ALL HE LOVED THE FALL
> THE LEAVES YELLOW ON THE
>   COTTONWOODS
> LEAVES FLOATING ON THE TROUT
>   STREAMS
> AND ABOVE THE HILLS
>   THE HIGH BLUE WINDLESS SKIES
> . . . NOW HE WILL BE A PART OF THEM
>   FOREVER

Index

Across the River and Into the Trees, 101, 114
Adams Gulch, 20, 30
Anderson, Don, 125, 154–55
Antelope (horse), 20, 104
Atkinson, Chuck, 128–29, 131, 158

Bergman, Ingrid, 96
Big Wood River, 20
Bilbao, Dan, 129
Boettiger, Anna Roosevelt, 71
Boettiger, John, 71
Brown, George, 158
Bruce, Toby, 32, 33, 36, 58–61, 107

Campbell, Frances, 126
Canoeing, 12–14
Capa, Robert, 50–55, 75
Chapin, Ellis, 40, 55, 56
Cooper, Bary, 25, 28, 40–47, 96–97, 119, 155

Daly, Ray, 24
Daugherty, Father, 38
Dunabeita, Juan, 94

Fishing, 12, 20
For Whom the Bell Tolls, 30, 33, 50, 73, 75, 131
Friede, Don, 50

Glamour House, 7, 22
Gellhorn, Martha, 2, 4, 6, 10, 28, 38–40, 56, 58
Geppart, Karl, 4
Gingrich, Arnold, 25
Gooding, Tom, 47

Hamilton, Bill, 19, 23, 47, 63
Hamilton, Ray, 62–63
Hannagan, Steve, 28
Harriman, Averell, 71–72
Harriman, Kathleen, 71
Hawks, Howard, 71, 73
Hayward, Leland, 71, 104
Hegstrom, Bud, 128
Hellinger, Mark, 81–85, 102
Hemingway, Betty, 86
Hemingway, Ernest, depression of, 153–60; family of, 6,
    31, 33–35, 50, 62, 75–77, 87–88, 104–105, 129–30,
    136–37, 146–48; hunting and, 6, 7–10, 22–26, 31–32,
    64–67, 87–88, 102–104, 107–14; wedding of, 55–56
Hemingway, Gregory, 36
Hemingway, Jack (Bumby), 36, 62, 75–77
Hemingway, Mary, 87–88, 104–105, 129–30, 136–37,
    146–48
Hemingway, Patrick, 36, 81
Hemingway, Pauline, 50
Herraras, Roberto, 94, 132
Higgon, Joan, 154

Hill, Pete, 104, 132, 138–39
Hunter, Vince, 120

Jankow, Les, 125
Johnson, Larry, 153–55
Jordan, Robert, 96

Kneeland, George, 128
Knight, Dan, 125

Lost River Mountains, 16–17

McCrea, Winston, 43
McGoldrick, Ray, 126
MacMullen, Forrest, 125
Mark, Pop, 20, 25, 125
Miles, Bob, 20, 33

Old Man and the Sea, The, 102, 104
Ordonez, Antonio, 132–34
Oregon Trail, 97

Pahsimeroi River Valley, 17
Perkins, Maxwell, 22
Pierce, Waldo, 129
PM magazine, 56
Purdy, Bud, 13, 87, 150

Redden, Jack, 62, 63–64, 125
Rogers, Pat, 1–2, 7

Saviers, Dr. George, 124, 130–31, 136, 142, 149, 153–55
Saviers, Pat, 124
Shoshoni Indians, 18
Silver Creek, 12, 25
Spackman, Spike, 20
Spiegel, Clara, 122
Stanwyck, Barbara, 71
Stewart, Stew, 38, 50
Sullavan, Margaret, 71
Sun Valley, 20
Sweeney, Charlie, 85

Taylor, Robert, 71
Tracy, Spencer, 104
Trail Creek Cabin, 73, 96
Topping, Bob, 128

Van Guilder, Gene, 1–4, 6–7, 12, 20, 25–30, 43
Van Guilder, Nin, 12, 29, 43

Welsh, Mary, 75–79
Williams, Bob, 124–25
Williams, Taylor, 7, 10–11, 22–23, 30–31, 38, 58, 67, 86,
    91–100, 114, 122–24
Womak, Ab, 29–30
Wood, Art, 62, 125